Gratefulness,
the Heart of Prayer

Gratefulness, the Heart of Prayer

An Approach to Life in Fullness

Brother David Steindl-Rast

Paulist Press 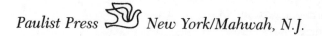 *New York/Mahwah, N.J.*

Cover design by Lynn Else

Library of Congress
Catalog Card Number: 84-60724

ISBN: 0-8091-2628-1

Published by Paulist Press
997 Macarthur Boulevard
Mahwah, New Jersey 07430

www.paulistpress.com

Printed and bound in the
United States of America

Contents

v

What counts is prayerfulness, not prayers. And the fullness of prayer is grateful living.

For all of us (not only for "contemplatives") the fullness of grateful life is contemplation: the art of living leisurely.

Gratefulness implies courageous trust in life (as "given"): the prayer of faith beyond beliefs—Living by the Word.

Gratefulness implies openness for the surprises in life: the prayer of hope beyond hopes—Prayer of Silence.

Gratefulness is an unconditional "yes" to life as give-and-take: the prayer of love beyond likes and dislikes—Contemplation in Action.

An ABC of grateful living: keywords as aids to the memory.

In gratefulness
I dedicate this book
to my Mother, my Brothers, and my Sisters
and to all without whom it could never have
been written.

Special thanks to Peter Stewart,
founder of the Center for World Thanksgiving
at Dallas, Texas, for urging me to write this
book and supporting me in doing so.

Mission Bay, New Zealand: June 13, 1983.

Brother David

Acknowledgments

Excerpts from *Four Quartets* by T.S. Eliot, copyright 1943 by T.S. Eliot, renewed 1971 by Esme Valerie Eliot, are reprinted by permission of Harcourt Brace Jovanovich, Inc. and Faber and Faber Ltd. The excerpt from *Trio in a Mirror* by Dorothy Donnelly, copyright © 1960, is reprinted by permission of the University of Arizona Press. Selections from *The Kabir Book* by Robert Bly, copyright © 1977 by Robert Bly, is used by permission of Beacon Press. Excerpts from "Winds," © 1955 by W.H. Auden, and "Precious Five," © 1950 by W.H. Auden, are taken from *W. H. Auden: Collected Poems,* edited by Edward Mendelson, and reprinted by permission of Random House, Inc. Excerpts from *Duino Elegies* by Ranier Maria Rilke, translated by J.B. Leishman and Stephen Spender, are reprinted by permission of W.W. Norton & Company, Inc., copyright 1939 by W.W. Norton & Company, Inc., copyright renewed 1967 by Stephen Spender and J.B. Leishman. The poem "Pax" is taken from *The Collected Poems of D.H. Lawrence,* collected and edited by Vivian de Sola Pinto and F. Warren Roberts, copyright © 1964, 1971 by Angelo Ravageli and C.M. Weekley, executors of the estate of Frieda Lawrence Ravageli, and reprinted by permission of Viking Penguin, Inc.

Foreword

This book is a true delight! It delights by its surprising insights, its unexpected perspectives and its gentle humor. When I finished reading it and put it down (or up!), with a grateful smile, I knew that I wanted to introduce the delightful monk who had written it, because many times, while moving through the pages, I said to myself: "How wonderful it would be if the reader could meet Brother David, the vibrant lively man who stands behind these delightful words about gratitude, joy, prayer and praise."

Knowing Brother David is a special grace. As long as I have been in the United States I have been blessed with his presence in my life. I have seldom taught a course without trying to make David a part of it, because I know that the thousands of people who hear him speak in churches, classrooms and retreat centers never forget him. Whenever he speaks, it always is much more than a brilliant lecture. It is something of an event. When Brother

David enters into the heart and mind of his listener something new happens to them and they know it.

Brother David is my ideal of a teacher. He not only offers stimulating ideas and good theories, but he also creates the climate in which these ideas and theories can be received without fear and then explored in the heart. He does much more than speak about the spiritual life—he speaks of it with the authority of the monk who is living it. For Brother David there hardly seems to be a distinction between teaching, preaching, praying and meditating. All of these for him are one process and he has the ability to invite his listeners to become part of his own experience, and to enter with him in the places that fill him with gratitude and joy. His lively gestures, his open, always surprised eyes, his attentiveness to every question, his concise responses, his sparkling humor and most of all his obvious love for his students allow him to open hearts that remain mostly closed to the realities from and about which he speaks. Often, students remark that after listening to David, they see clearly what until then they had not been able to understand. To my embarrassment, I discovered that concepts I had explored elaborately in the same course became suddenly and unexpectedly crystal clear when Brother David touched upon them. My embarrassment, however, was always a happy embarrassment since I too experienced that same clarity and felt loved in a new way that freed me to understand with less fear.

One of the most remarkable qualities of Brother David's teaching is his ability to make old words new. To very simple and "normal" words such as joy, peace, patience, humility, obedience, heart and mind he is able to give such a fresh tone that it seems as if he uses them for the first time. He speaks them with so much care that they appear as precious gifts to be admired and joyfully shared with others. Thus his words are always more than just words. They become active instruments of inner transformation. They give you a glimpse of the mystery that God's word became flesh not only two thousand years ago but every time we truly listen.

Gratefulness, the Heart of Prayer is the precious fruit of many years of teaching. Those who have met Brother David will see his gestures and hear his voice and feel his presence on every page of this book. Those who as yet do not know him will sense that the words written here come from a place which every true searcher for the truth wants to go. It is the place of careful listening, quiet joy and solid peace.

Although this book deals with most of the aspects of the spiritual life and speaks about faith, hope and love as its core, gratefulness is the theme that sets the tone of all that is written. With Brother David as the author it could hardly be different. Brother David's monastic life has formed him in gratitude. He knows with his heart and mind that a monk is a monk to say thanks. "The human heart is made for universal praise," he writes and as a monk he wants to make this truth visible in his concrete daily life.

Whenever Brother David came to visit me he surprised me with his gratefulness—not just gratefulness for what I or others did or said but gratefulness for the many gifts that I had come to take for granted. He saw flowers with an expression of discovery and surprise, he looked at the sky as a marvelous piece of art, he admired poetry, music and handicrafts with a spontaneous enthusiasm, and he kept discovering endless new occasions to say thanks and offer praise to his God who keeps showering him with new gifts.

In the midst of a pragmatic world in which we constantly ask ourselves how useful things—and even people—are, Brother David calls us to "useless" praise. In the midst of a world in which hatred, strife, violence, and war dominate our consciousness, Brother David points our eyes in another direction and tells us that joy and peace are closer at hand than we might realize. In the midst of a world in which fear, apprehension and suspicion make us live stingy, narrow and small lives, Brother David stretches out his arms, smiles and says: "Love wholeheartedly, be surprised, give thanks and praise— then you will discover the fullness of your life."

Gratefulness, the Heart of Prayer is indeed a delightful book. It throws a ray of light in our dark world and makes us see that we can live here and now as people who can be constantly surprised and who can let an "inch of surprise become a mile of gratefulness."

Henri J.M. Nouwen

Aliveness and Wakefulness
(In place of an Introduction)

This book is about life in fullness. It is about coming
alive. I could summarize it in two words: <u>Wake up</u>!

A poet like Kabir is able to say these two words
with a freshness that makes us sit up. Kabir's poems
have power. They wake us up to an aliveness we
never thought possible.

> Do you have a body? Don't sit on the porch!
> Go out and walk in the rain!
>
> If you are in love,
> then why are you asleep?
>
> Wake up, wake up!
> You have slept millions and millions of years.
> Why not wake up this morning?

In my own way, I try to get the same message
across. And people are hungry for it. All around the

world I have been invited to speak about it. And people always ask, "Why don't you write this down?" That's what I have done here.

Of what use is an introduction? A few readers will skim it. The rest will skip it altogether. The skippers won't read this anyway. For skimmers I have a suggestion. There is an alphabetical list of key words at the end of this book. You might want to glance at that list. If I haven't completely failed, it will show you two things:

1. Waking up is a continuing process. No one wakes up once and for all. There is no limit to wakefulness, just as there is no limit to aliveness.
2. It is risky to be awake to life. It takes courage.

We have to choose between risk and risk. We run the risk of sleeping through life, of never waking up at all. Or else we wakefully rise to the risk of life, facing the challenge of life, of love.

> If you are in love,
> then why are you asleep?

Men and women who dare face this question may find this book helpful. For others, reading it would be a waste of time. As Kabir put it:

> If you are about to fall into heavy sleep anyway,
> why waste time smoothing the bed
> and arranging the pillows?

Surprise and Gratefulness

A rainbow always comes as a surprise. Not that it cannot be predicted. Surprising sometimes means unpredictable, but it often means more. Surprising in the full sense means somehow gratuitous. Even the predictable turns into surprise the moment we stop taking it for granted. If we knew enough, everything would be predictable, and yet everything would remain gratuitous. If we knew how the whole universe worked, we would still be surprised that there was a universe at all. Predictable it may be, yet all the more surprising.

Our eyes are opened to that surprise character of the world around us the moment we wake up from taking things for granted. Rainbows have a way of waking us up. A complete stranger might pull your sleeve and point to the sky: "Did you notice the rainbow?" Bored and boring adults become excited children. We might not even understand what it was that startled us when we saw that rainbow. What was it? Gratuitousness burst in on us,

9

the gratuitousness of all there is. When this happens, our spontaneous response is surprise. Plato recognized that surprise as the beginning of philosophy. It is also the beginning of gratefulness.

A close brush with death can trigger that surprise. For me, that came early in life. Growing up in Nazi-occupied Austria, I knew air raids from daily experience. And an air raid can be an eye-opener. One time, I remember, the bombs started falling as soon as the warning sirens went off. I was on the street. Unable to find an air raid shelter quickly, I rushed into a church only a few steps away. To shield myself from shattered glass and falling debris, I crawled under a pew and hid my face in my hands. But as bombs exploded outside and the ground shook under me, I felt sure that the vaulted ceiling would cave in any moment and bury me alive. Well, my time had not yet come. A steady tone of the siren announced that the danger was over. And there I was, stretching my back, dusting off my clothes, and stepping out into a glorious May morning. I was alive. Surprise! The buildings I had seen less than an hour ago were now smoking mounds of rubble. But that there was anything at all struck me as an overwhelming surprise. My eyes fell on a few square feet of lawn in the midst of all this destruction. It was as if a friend had offered me an emerald in the hollow of his hand. Never before or after have I seen grass so surprisingly green.

Surprise is no more than a beginning of that fullness we call gratefulness. But a beginning it is.

Do we find it difficult to imagine that gratefulness could ever become our basic attitude toward life? In moments of surprise we catch at least a glimpse of the joy to which gratefulness opens the door. More than that—in moments of surprise we already have a foot in the door. There are some who claim not to know gratefulness. But is there anyone who never knew surprise? Does springtime not surprise us anew each year, or that expanse of the bay opening up as we come around the bend of the road? Is it not a surprise each time we drive that way?

Things and events that trigger surprise are merely catalysts. I started with rainbows because they do the trick for most of us, but there are more personal catalysts. We have to find our own, each one of us. No matter how often that cardinal comes for the cracked corn scattered on a rock for the birds in winter, it is a flash of surprise. I expect him. I've come to even know his favorite feeding times. I can hear him chirping long before he comes in sight. But when that red streak shoots down on the rock like lightning on Elijah's altar, I know what e.e. cummings means: "The eyes of my eyes are opened."

Once we wake up in this way, we can strive to stay awake. Then we can allow ourselves to become more and more awakened. Waking up is a process. In the morning it is quite a different process for different people. Some of us wake up with a start and are wide awake for the rest of the day. They are lucky. Others have to do it stage by stage, cup of coffee by cup of coffee. What counts is that we don't go back to bed again. What counts on your path to fulfillment is that we remember the great truth that moments of surprise want to teach us: everything is gratuitous, everything is gift. The degree to which we are awake to this truth is the measure of our gratefulness. And gratefulness is the measure of our aliveness. Are we not dead to whatever we take for granted? Surely to be numb is to be dead. For those who awaken to life through surprise, death lies behind, not ahead. To live life open for surprise, in spite of all the dying which living implies, makes us ever more alive.

There are degrees of grateful wakefulness. Our intellect, our will, our emotions must wake up. Let us take a closer look at this process of awakening. It is the growth process of gratefulness.

A single crocus blossom ought to be enough to convince our heart that springtime, no matter how predictable, is somehow a gift, gratuitous, gratis, a grace. We know this with a knowledge that goes beyond our intellect. Yet our intellect shares in it. We cannot be grateful unless our intellect plays its role. We must recognize the gift as gift, and only our intellect can do that.

For some people this is not easy. There are those who are simply too dull, too slow witted, perhaps too lazy to recognize anything as gift. Their intellect is not alert enough. They take everything for granted. They go through life in a daze. It takes a certain intellectual sharpness to be grateful. But there are those with the opposite bent of mind, people who rely exclusively on their intellect. Those clever ones, too, may have a hard time with gratefulness. If one's intellect insists on finding solid proof that a gift is truly a gift, then one is stuck. There is always the possibility that what looks like a gift is really a trap, a bait, a bribe. Just listen to some of the comments one hears as Christmas presents are being unwrapped. "Well, look at this! Why would the Joneses send us an expensive present like this? I wonder what favor they are going to ask from us in the new year!" Who can prove that there are absolutely no strings attached? Our heart longs for the surprise that a gift is truly a free gift. But our proud intellect balks at surprise, wants to explain it, wants to explain it away.

Intellect by itself only gets us so far. It has a share in gratefulness, but only a share. Our intellect should be alert enough to look through the predictable husks of things to their core and find there a kernel of surprise. That in itself is a demanding task. But truthfulness also demands that the intellect be sufficiently humble, that is, sufficiently down to earth to know its limits. The gift character of everything can be recognized, but it cannot be proved— not by the intellect alone, at any rate. Proof lies in living. And there is more to living than the intellect can grasp.

Our will also must play its part. It too belongs to the fullness of gratefulness. It is the task of the intellect to recognize something as a gift, but the will must acknowledge its gift character. Recognition and acknowledgement are two different tasks. We can recognize something against our will. The will may refuse to acknowledge what the intellect sees. Awakened by surprise, we can recognize that what we call a "given" world is truly given. For we have not made it, earned it, or deserved it; chances are that we have not even fully approved of it. What confronts us is a given reality, and we recognize it as given. But only if we acknowledge this gift will our recognition lead to gratefulness. And acknowledging a gift may be far more difficult than recognizing it.

For example, take the weather. Everyone is aware that the weather on a given day is a given fact, and no amount of complaining about it will change it. But it makes a difference whether we merely recognize the weather as a given fact or willingly accept it as, in fact, given—that is, as gift. W.H. Auden observes:

> . . . weather
> Is what nasty people are
> Nasty about, and the nice
> Show a common joy in observing.

In recognizing what kind of weather we've got, the nice and the nasty agree. But from there on they part company. What makes the nice ones joyful? They are like children unwrapping a gift. But the nasty ones won't acknowledge it as gift.

Why is it so difficult to acknowledge a gift as gift? Here is the reason. When I admit that something is a gift, I admit my dependence on the giver. This may not sound that difficult, but there is something within us that bristles at the idea of dependence. We want to get along by ourselves. Yet a gift is something we simply cannot give to ourselves— not as a gift, at any rate. I can buy the same thing or even something better. But it will not be a gift if I procure it for myself. I can go out and treat myself to a magnificent treat. I can even be grateful later for the good time I had. But can I be grateful to myself for having treated myself so well? That would be neck-breaking mental acrobatics. Gratefulness always goes beyond myself. For what makes something a gift is precisely that it is given. And the receiver depends on the giver.

This dependence is always there when a gift is given and received. Even a mother depends on her child for the smallest gift. Suppose a little boy buys his mother a bunch of daffodils. He is giving nothing that he has not already received. His mother gave him not only the money he spent, but his very life and the upbringing that made him generous. Yet his gift is something that she depends on his giving. There is no other way she could receive it as a gift. And she finds more joy in that dependence than in the gift itself. Gift giving is a celebration of the bond that unites giver and receiver. That bond is gratefulness.

When I acknowledge a gift received, I acknowledge a bond that binds me to the giver. But we tend to fear the obligations this bond entails. When I learned English thirty years ago, it was current usage in America to express one's thanks by saying "very much obliged." Hardly anyone uses that expression today. Why not? We simply do not want to be obliged. We want to be self-sufficient. Our language gives us away.

There is, of course, a healthy side to our desire for independence. We want to fend for ourselves. Without that desire we would not outgrow the stage of being spoon-fed. And to outgrow that state we had to go through the phase of ending a meal with oatmeal on our nose, chin, ears, and bib. But even after we have learned to feed ourselves, it might be assumed that we would still have sense enough to let a nurse feed us if that became necessary. To grow up means learning to help ourselves, but also to accept help when we need it. Some people never seem to grow beyond the state of "let me do it alone." But compassionate eyes see through the outer stubborn independence and recognize within a child in a high chair, with oatmeal from head to toe.

In a sense, it is correct to fear dependence. Mere dependence is slavery. But independence is an illusion. If we really had to choose between dependence and independence, we would be in trouble. The choice is actually between alienation and interdependence. Independence is alienation. It cuts us off from others. But mere dependence, in a subtle way, is alienation too. For mere dependence is slavery; and the slave is an alien. But interdependence joins us with others through the bond of a joyful give-and-take, a bond of belonging. Dependence ties us with ties of slavery. Independence ties us with ties of illusion. But the bonds of interdependence are ties that set us free. One single gift acknowledged in gratefulness has power to dissolve the ties of our alienation, and we are home free— home where all depend on all.

The interdependence of gratefulness is truly mutual. The receiver of the gift depends on the giver. Obviously so. But the circle of gratefulness is incomplete until the giver of the gift becomes the receiver: a receiver of thanks. When we give thanks, we give something greater than the gift we received, whatever it was. The greatest gift one can give is thanksgiving. In giving gifts, we give what we can spare, but in giving thanks we give ourselves. One who says "Thank you" to another really says, "We belong together." Giver and thanksgiver belong together. The bond that unites them frees them from alienation. Does our society suffer from so much alienation because we fail to cultivate gratefulness?

The moment I acknowledge the gift as gift and so acknowledge my dependence, I am free—free to go forward into full gratefulness. This fullness comes with the joy of appreciating the gift. Appreciation is a response of our feelings. Our intellect recognizes the gift as a gift, our will acknowledges it, but only our feelings respond with joy and so fully appreciate the gift.

Many years ago I saw a photograph I would never forget: two African children smiling their radiant smiles. And the caption read, "Joy is the gratefulness of God's children." Later, when I traveled in Africa, I rediscovered that smile and the caption came back to me. Everywhere in the world joy is the true expression of gratefulness. But not everywhere are the faces of God's children as transparent to that joy as in black Africa. Nowhere have I seen more radiant joy in children's eyes than in the former Biafra. In Enugu I came across groups of children who gather on a busy street corner after dark, set up a small altar, and pray the rosary undisturbed by the hustle and bustle of adults around them. Children, I was told, started that custom during the bloodiest weeks of the war. One generation of children has handed it on to the next for more than a decade. Then it dawned on me that the joy I observed plays on a deep knowledge of suffering as sunrays play on the surface of dark waterholes. Only a heart familiar with death will appreciate the gift of life with so deep a feeling of joy.

We will later explore the meaning of "heart" in the context of thankfulness. Then, I trust, it will become clearer why intellect, will, and emotions, all three, must be engaged in thanksgiving. All three belong to the full notion of "heart." All three belong, therefore, also to the notion of gratefulness.

Thanksgiving is a gesture of the whole heart, or it is nothing.

We saw that our intellect must steer a straight course between dullness and sophistication in order to recognize the given world as truly a gift. And soon we realize how difficult this straightforward simplicity is for our complex, twisted minds. Our will must stay clear of both compulsive self-sufficiency and slavish dependence in order to freely acknowledge the bond that the gift establishes. This, too, is quickly recognized as a difficult task. But when we consider the role our feelings play in appreciating the gift, nothing seems easier. And yet here, too, we have to avoid two traps in order to find that childlike, free response in which our feelings resonate with gratefulness.

One of the two traps in which our feelings can get caught turns us into a wallflower, the other into a vampire. The vampire in us cannot fully enjoy the dance because it is too eager; the wallflower can't because it doesn't dare. One squeezes the last drop of feeling out of every experience. The other's feelings have been hurt too often. But the child in us steps out, self-forgetful, spontaneous, with the graceful gesture of gratefulness.

We know the extent to which we are inclined to grab and snatch at life's gifts. We are well aware of the first trap. When we recall how vulnerable our feelings are, we become aware of the second trap, too. Never are we more vulnerable than in those moments when we respond from the heart. For moments of gratitude are those in which we open our heart and are thus more easily wounded.

For instance, recall this situation. You notice someone smiling at you; gratefully you acknowledge the smile by smiling back. Then something does not seem quite right. You turn around and notice that behind you stands someone for whom that smile was actually meant. It hurts, doesn't it? No big trauma, of course. But we can imagine that someone whose feelings were hurt repeatedly, especially during childhood, may be permanently injured. The person may have frequently acknowledged gifts that turned out to be either no gifts at all, or gifts meant for someone else. Gradually emotional scar tissue developed, making feeling responses clumsy and painful. The person may need help in the exercise of feelings so as to become nimble again. This is an emotional counterpart to physiotherapy.

Intellect, will, and emotions—each has a special role to play, and all three must harmonize in whole-hearted gratefulness. We can now go a step further and ask: How can we become more grateful? We shall again focus in turn on intellect, will, and emotions as we look for ways of growing in gratitude. The first thing to remember is to start where we are. How could we start where we are not? And yet, how often we try to start way ahead of ourselves! That leads nowhere. But wherever we are, help is there. Life provides all the help we need. If we trust and look for it, we shall find it. Life is full of surprises. And surprise is the key to gratefulness.

?
not
really

No matter how dull or intellectually trapped we are, surprise is close at hand. Even when our life lacks the surprise of the extraordinary, the ordinary always wants to surprise us afresh. As a friend wrote to me from Minnesota on a winter morning: "I got up before dawn and caught God painting all the trees white. He's been doing much of His best work while we sleep to surprise us when we get up."

It is like the surprise we found in our rainbow. We can learn to let our sense of surprise be triggered not only by the extraordinary, but, above all, by a fresh look at the ordinary. "Nature is never spent," says Gerard Manley Hopkins in praise of God's grandeur. "There lives the dearest freshness deep down things." The surprise of the unexpected will wear off, but the surprise of that freshness never wears off. In rainbows it is obvious. Less obvious, the surprise of freshness is present in the most ordinary things. We can learn to see it as plainly as we see the powdery bloom on fresh blueberries, "a mist from the breath of a wind," as Robert Frost calls it, "a tarnish that goes at the touch of a hand."

We can train ourselves to see that bloom of surprise by spotting it first where it's easiest for us to find. The child in us always remains alive, open for surprise, never ceasing to be amazed at something or other. It may be that I saw "this morning morning's minion," Gerard Manley Hopkins' "dapple-dawn-drawn falcon in his riding," or simply it may be this morning's inch of toothpaste on my brush. Both are equally amazing to the eyes of the heart, for the greatest surprise is that there is anything at all—that we are here. We can cultivate our intellect's taste for surprise. And whatever causes us to look with amazement opens "the eyes of our eyes." We begin to see everything as a gift. An inch of surprise can lead to miles of gratefulness.

Surprise leads us on the path of gratefulness. This is true not only for our intellect, but also for our will. No matter how tenaciously our will clings to self-sufficiency, life provides the help we need to get out of that trap. Self-sufficiency is an illusion. And, sooner or later, life shatters every illusion. None of us would be what we are if it were not for our parents, teachers, and friends. Even our enemies help make us what we are. There never was a self-made person. Every one of us needs others. Sooner or later life brings this truth home to us. By a sudden bereavement, by a long lingering sickness, or in some other way, life catches us by surprise. Catches us? Frees us by surprise, I should say. Painful it may be, but pain is a small price to pay for freedom from self-deception.

Self-sufficiency is self-deception on a still deeper level. Our true Self is not the little individual self over against other selves. We discover this in moments when, to our surprise, we experience deep communion with all other beings. These moments occur in everyone's life. We may remember them as high-water marks of awareness, of aliveness, of being at our best and most truly ourselves. Or we may try to suppress the memory of those moments because that springtide of communion threatens the defensive isolation in which we feel snug. The walls behind which we hide may resist life's battering for a long time. But, suddenly one day, the great surprise will break in on us, as in the following account from *The Protean Body* by Don Johnson.

> ... I walked out onto a dock in the Gulf of Mexico. *I* ceased to exist. I experienced being a part of the sea breeze, the movement of the water and the fish, the light rays cast by the sun, the colors of the palms and tropical flowers. I had no sense of past or future. It was not a particularly blissful experience: it was terrifying. It was the kind of ecstatic experience I'd invested a lot of energy in avoiding.
>
> I did not experience myself as the *same* as the water, the wind, and the light, but as participating with them in the same system of movement. We were all dancing together. . . .

In this great dance, giver and receiver are one. We suddenly realize how little it matters which of the two roles one happens to play at a given time. Beyond time, our true self rests in itself in perfect stillness. Within time, this is realized by a graceful give-and-take in the dance of life. As in a fast spinning top, the stillness and the dance are one. Only in that oneness is true self-sufficiency. Any other self-sufficiency is illusion. But the real is stronger in the end than any illusion. Sooner or later it will shine through like the sun through fog. Life, our teacher, will see to that.

Sometimes we express compulsive independence by a constant eagerness to help others while refusing any help we ourselves might need. If this should be the case, let's, here too, start where we are. Let's ask: What would I do if there were no one who needed my help? The helper needs the helpless as much as the helpless needs the helper. Help is not a one-way street, but a give-and-take. Let us continue then to enjoy helping as we have done before but add to it a new joy that arises when we acknowledge and accept our own need to be needed. Once we have tasted the flavor of this joy, we shall find it everywhere. For wherever we may be, we are in some way engaged in a universal give-and-take.

If our feelings are too scarred or too jaded to fully vibrate with this great giving and receiving, we might at least find one small area in which we spontaneously respond with joy. That is our starting point. Here again: Where we are, not where we'd want to be, is where we must begin. And here, too, surprise can become the igniting spark. What is it that makes you feel good? Physical exercise? Harmony at home? A chance to help others? Whatever it may be, surprise lies at its root. Whenever our feelings touch that "freshness deep down things," they thrill with youthful joy. If we begin by fully tasting joy where at this time we can, wider and wider areas of our feelings will become youthful again and respond. Gratefulness makes us young. By growing more grateful, we grow younger every day. Why not?

Let me sum up. Surprise is the starting point. Through surprise our inner eyes are opened to the amazing fact that everything is gratuitous. Nothing at all can be taken for granted. And if it cannot be taken for granted, it is gift. That is the weighty meaning of the expression we use so lightly when we speak of "a given world." What we have mostly in mind when we speak of a given situation, a given fact, a given world, is that we cannot change it. But that can hardly be called mind*ful* (with emphasis on full). What we should also have in mind when we call something "given" is that it is a gift. True mindfulness gets that gift aspect of the world into view. When our intellect learns to recognize the gift aspect of the world, when our will learns to acknowledge it, our feelings to appreciate it, ever wider circles of mindfulness make our world come alive. I have in mind the image of expanding ripples on the surface of a pond. The pebble that started them off is the little plop of surprise. As the ripples expand, we come alive. In the end, gratefulness will be our full aliveness to a gratuitously given world.

Heart and Mind

Gratefulness is a mindful response, as we have seen. Our intellect, our will, our feelings are all engaged when we are grateful. But when we say mindful, someone might still get the impression that we want to stress the mind over against the rest of our person. It might be less misleading to speak of the heart rather than the mind. Gratefulness is a full response. We sense that. And we sense also that this kind of fullness cannot go together with halfheartedness. Gratefulness is always wholehearted. Our whole person is engaged in it. And this is precisely what the symbol of the heart stands for—the whole person.

When lovers say to one another, "I will give you my heart," they do not mean, "I will give you *part* of myself." Not even the best part will do. What they want to say is that they are willing to give themselves, all of themselves, their innermost being. More than that: the heart is not a static symbol. It is dynamic, alive. The heart is the pulsating core of our aliveness in more than merely the physical sense. To say "I will give you my heart" is to say, "I will give you my life." Gratefulness is full aliveness, and that very aliveness is summed up in the symbol of the heart. All of my past history, all of my future possibilities, this heartbeat in the present moment holds all of it together.

The key word for speaking of the heart is "together." The heart is center of our being where intellect and will and feelings, mind and body, past and future come together. When we discover that spot where our life holds together, we discover the heart. That is why I call the heart the taproot of the whole person. When we grasp the taproot of a dandelion to be pulled, or of a dogwood tree to be transplanted, we know that we have taken hold of the whole plant. And there are moments when something touched that very root of our being. It went to our heart.

We all remember times when something took hold of our heart. We know from experience that such moments of wholehearted mindfulness are moments of blissful wholeness, of communion, moments when we feel one with all. What triggers this sudden self-discovery of our heart may be a weighty decision, a blow of fate that hits us hard, a memorable encounter, a long-awaited event. But more often what stirs us so deeply will be a surprisingly small matter, an everyday occurrence, something done a hundred times before. There seems to be no reason why at the hundred and first time it should move us so amazingly, but it does. A mother looks at her baby asleep in the crib every afternoon, yet today the sight floods her whole heart with a gratefulness too deep for words. Or you drive a stretch of highway you pass twice a day, yet this time the hum of the car, the red and white flags at the used car lot, the very ordinariness of the moment seizes your heart with extraordinary power.

It is almost impossible to capture such high points of aliveness in words. But words can point to them and stir up memories. What one remembers most about these moments of the heart is a deep, all-pervading, overflowing sense of gratefulness. This gratefulness is not the same as thanksgiving. It gives rise to thanksgiving, but it lies deeper. Even before it bursts forth into thanks to God or to life, the experience deserves the name gratefulness because it is one's full response to a gratuitously given moment. When those two come together, gratuitousness and fullness, one is suddenly together. One is responding from the heart, from that center where all is together.

Remembering such moments of the heart, we can easily see that "together" is a word that fits. The experience pulls us together at a deep level. But remembering the experience will in turn help us realize that the word "together" means here a great deal more than we might have suspected. We are together with ourselves at our heart of hearts in a full and deep sense, but so fully and so deeply that this also means being together with everyone else.

When we reach our innermost heart, we reach a realm where we are not only intimately at home with ourselves, but intimately united with others, all others. The heart is not a lonely place. It is the realm where solitude and togetherness coincide. Our own experience proves this, does it not? Can one ever say, "Now I am truly together with myself, yet I remain alienated from others"? Or could one say, "I am truly together with others, or even just with one other person I love, yet I remain alienated from myself"? Unthinkable! The moment we are one with ourselves, we are one with all others. We have overcome alienation. And the heart stands for that core of being where, long before alienation, primordial togetherness held sway.

Those are the two poles of our most basic choice: alienation and togetherness, synonyms for sin and salvation. "Sin" is a word that has lost much of its usefulness today. Too many people just do not understand that term anymore. And what is the point of using a language that is more likely than not to be misunderstood? But when I say "alienation" everyone knows what I mean. The term suggests to our experience today something that is practically identical with what one used to call "sin" in the past. Togetherness, on the other hand, is what our whole being longs for. An older vocabulary called it "salvation." "Salvation" used to have that sense of an all-embracing wholeness which the word "together" suggests to us. In our innermost heart we know that wholeness is more basic, more primordial than alienation, and so we never quite lose an inborn trust that in the end we shall be whole and together.

The German poet Rainer Maria Rilke celebrates both our longing for healing and wholeness and our primordial conviction that God's healing power wells up in our own innermost heart. He finds God in "the spot that is healing," while we, like children picking on a scar, keep ripping it open with the sharp edges of our thoughts. If only we could quiet all that agitation within and around us, the din that distracts us. In our silence a thousand scattered thoughts would be gathered into one. And in the thousandfold power of that concentration we would be able to hold God one smiling moment long in a single thought. Just long enough to give that divine Presence away to all life. And what form would we find for that giving? Rilke's answer is thanksgiving.

> Oh, if for once all were completely still!
> If all mere happenstance and chance
> were silenced, and the laughter next door, too;
> if all that droning of my senses
> did not prevent my being wide awake—
>
> Then, with one thousandfold thought,
> I would reach your horizon
> and, for the span of a smile, hold you
> to give you away to all life
> as thanksgiving.

This prayer rings true to us because our heart holds the pledge, as it were, of a primordial promise.

Its fulfillment would mean being one and whole within myself. It would mean being one with all others in peaceful communion. Thus, it would mean no less than finding my true and all-embracing Self. But it would mean still more. When we really find our heart, we find the realm where we are intimately one with self, with others, and also with God. Yes, that is the most amazing discovery: that in the depth of my heart, to borrow St. Augustine's words, "God is closer to me than I am to myself."

When the Bible tells how God creates us human beings by breathing life into us, this intimate communion with God is seen as the core of our being human. We are alive with God's own life. The heart, the center of our aliveness, is then also the focal point of our communion with God. The heart is where we meet God. But meeting God is prayer. And so we know one more thing about the heart: it is our meeting place with God in prayer. Prayer, in turn, is the very heart of religion.

We should not talk, however, as if it were perfectly clear what one means by God, by prayer, or even by religion. Today these words mean different things to different people. What do they mean to you? As soon as we try to give an account, we may find that we are pretty vague in our notions. Out of intellectual honesty, then, let us make sure that, for our purpose here at least, we know what we mean by our key concepts. And since "religion" is the most basic term when we try to understand the heart, let's start with "religion."

There is something about the heart which everyone knows from experience, and which we have not yet mentioned. "Restless is our heart." That is how St. Augustine put it. The core of our being is relentlessly questioning, searching, longing. The very beating of the heart within my chest seems merely the echo of a restless pounding more deeply within me, a knocking on some locked door. It is not even clear to me: do I knock to get in, or do I knock to get out? But one thing is certain: restless is our heart. And that existential restlessness is what makes religion religious.

A particular religion merely provides a framework for the quest of the heart. Within each religion there are countless ways of being religious. In a personal quest we must find our own. No one can do it for us. This or that religion may provide the historical, cultural, sociological setting. It may provide an interpretation for our experience, a language to speak about it. If we are lucky, it may even provide incentives to keep us awake and alert in our quest and offer channels to protect its driving force from trickling away, from petering out. All this is of immeasurable value. Yet it remains on the outside. The heart of every religion is the religion of the heart.

"Restless is our heart until. . ." Until what? Until we find rest. But what can still our existential thirst? "As a deer yearns for running streams, so does my soul thirst for God, the living God" (Ps 42:2). Lucky the psalmist who could give a name to what our thirst is yearning for. But what name should we use now? Today many whose thirst is no less burning will not use the name "God" because of those of us who do use it. We have abused it and confused them. Can we find another name for that which gives rest to our heart? The term "meaning" suggests itself. When we find meaning in life, then we find rest. At least this is the starting point for an answer. But let us now assume that we know what meaning means. All we know is that we find rest when we find something meaningful. That is a matter of experience, and it is all we know about meaning. Meaning is simply that within which we find rest.

But so is the heart. It seems to be a contradiction. Yet our restless heart is also the only place where we find rest when, "at the end of all our exploring," we arrive where we started "and know the place for the first time." To know the heart means to know that it has depths too deep for reason to fathom, the depths of divine life within us. The heart that comes to rest in God rests in its own fathomless depth.

Here, another prayer from Rilke's *Book of Hours* allows these intuitions to crystallize into poetic images. Once more Rilke starts out with the polarity of noise and silence. This time it is the crowd of contradictions in our life that fills the palace of our heart with a riotous feast of fools. It is impossible, of course, to eliminate contradictions altogether from our life. Life itself is contradictory. But we can reconcile contradictions in the great primordial symbols, like the symbol of the heart itself. When we succeed in this, a great silence begins to reign, serenely festive and gentle. And in the middle of that silence stands God, as guest, as silent core of our soliloquies, as temporal center of a circle whose periphery goes beyond time.

> Whoever reconciles the many contradictions of his
>   life,
> gratefully gathering them into one symbol,
> expels the noisy crowd from his abode
> and in a different kind of festive mood
> receives you as his guest on gentle evenings.
>
> You are the Other in his solitude,
> a silent center for his conversations with himself,
> and every circle drawn around you
> makes his compass span beyond the rim of time.

When our heart rests in the Source of all meaning, it can encompass all meaning. Meaning, in this sense, is not something that can be put in words. Meaning is not something that can be looked up in a book, like a definition. Meaning is not something that can be grasped, held, stored away. Meaning is not something.... Maybe we should stop the sentence there. Meaning is no thing. It is more like the light in which we see things. Another Psalm calls out to God in the thirst of the heart: "With you is the fountain of life, and in your light we see light" (Ps 36:9). In thirsting for the fullness of life, our heart thirsts for the light that lets us see life's meaning. When we find meaning, we know it because our heart finds rest. It is always through our heart that we find meaning. Just as our eyes respond to light and our ears to sound, so our heart responds to meaning. The organ for meaning is the heart.

This suggests a religious vocabulary based on experience, based on the way we experience the world today. And our religious experience begins and ends with the heart. It begins with the insight that our heart is restless. A world of things can never fully satisfy its restless quest. Only that no-thing beyond all things that we call meaning gives us rest when we glimpse it. The quest of the human heart for meaning is the heartbeat of every religion.

Poetry gets this point across more convincingly because it appeals to a deep self-understanding of the human heart. Let me, therefore, quote once more one of Rilke's prayers. Here the poet gives free reign to his imagination. He envisions flamboyant gestures by which he would celebrate God's limitless Presence if he lived in a world of unlimited possibilities. But then in the last stanza he hesitates and, on second thought, comes up with an image that reaches deeper.

If I had grown up in a different world
where days are light and hours slender,
I would have planned a festival for you.
And there my hands would never hold you as they
do now, when I hold you fearfully and hard.

There, daringly I would have squandered you,
you limitless Presence.
Like a ball I would have tossed you
into the billowing joys
so that someone leaping,
hands lifted high towards your falling,
Should catch you,
you Thing of Things.

I would have let you flash
like a sword's blade.
In a ring of pure gold
I would have given your fire its setting
to hold it over the whitest hand.

I would have painted you: not on a screen
but on the very sky from verge to verge
like a giant would fashion you, so would I
have fashioned you: a mountain, a blaze,
a whirlwind rising from desert sands—

or
it may have happened: I found you
one time . . .
My friends are far away.
I hardly hear their laughter any more,
and you, you have fallen out of the nest.
You are a fledgling with yellow claws
and big eyes, and it hurts to see you so.
(My hand is far too broad for you.)
And I take with my fingers a drop from the spring.
I strain to see if you will take it with gaping beak.

I feel your heart throbbing and my own heart, too,
and both from fright.

All ways of being religious start from the heart
and end with the heart. The restlessness of the heart
leads from the misery of being alienated (often in
the midst of pleasure) to the joy of being together
with self, with all, with God (often in the midst of
suffering). "Together" is the word that marks the
goal of the religious quest. To find meaning means
finding how all belongs together and to find one's
place in that universal belonging. And that means
finding the heart. T. S. Eliot says:

> We shall not cease from exploration
> And the end of all our exploring
> Will be to arrive where we started
> And know the place for the first time.

When I discover that in my heart of hearts God is
closer to me than I am to myself, then I have come
home. When the thirsting heart discovers the fountain of life in its own unfathomable depth, then we
"arrive where we started and know the place for the
first time."

In prayer the heart drinks from the fountain of
meaning. In this sense, prayer is the heart of religion. We shall have to explore what that means. We
shall need to examine the practical implications of
what we merely touched upon in these remarks

about the heart. But this much should be clear so far: when we speak of the heart, we mean wholeness, fullness—the fullness of our being alive, the fullness implied by gratefulness and by prayerfulness.

Prayers and Prayerfulness

May we presume that everyone knows what prayer is? From one point of view the answer is "yes." Every human being knows prayer from experience. Have we not all experienced moments in which our thirsting heart found itself with surprise drinking at a fountain of meaning? Much of our life may be a wandering in desert lands, but we do find springs of water. If what is called "God" means in the language of experience the ultimate Source of Meaning, then those moments that quench the thirst of the heart are moments of prayer. They are moments when we communicate with God, and that is, after all, the essence of prayer.

But do we recognize these meaningful moments as prayer? Here, the answer is often "no." And under this aspect we cannot presume that everyone knows what prayer is. It happens that people who are in the habit of saying prayers at certain set times have their moments of genuine prayer precisely at times when they are not saying prayers. In fact, they may not even recognize their most prayer-ful moments as prayer. Others who never say formal prayers are nourished by moments of deep prayer-fulness. Yet, they would be surprised to learn that they are praying at all.

Suppose, for example, you are reciting Psalms. If all goes well, this may be a truly prayerful experi-ence. But all doesn't always go well. While reciting Psalms, you might experience nothing but a struggle against distractions. Half an hour later you are wa-tering your African violets. Now, suddenly the prayerfulness that never came during the prayers overwhelms you. You come alive from within. Your heart expands and embraces those velvet leaves, those blossoms looking up to you. The watering and drinking become a give-and-take so intimate that you cannot separate your pouring of the water from the roots' receiving, the flower's giving of joy from your drinking it in. And in a rush of gratefulness your heart celebrates this belonging together. As long as this lasts, everything has meaning, every-thing makes sense. You are communicating with your full self, with all there is, with God. Which was the real prayer, the Psalms or the watering of your African violets?

Sooner or later we discover that prayers are not always prayer. That is a pity. But the other half of that insight is that prayer often happens without any prayers. And that should cheer us up. In fact, it is absolutely necessary to distinguish between prayer and prayers. At least if we want to do what Scripture tells us to do and "pray continually" (Lk 18:1) we must distinguish praying from saying prayers. Otherwise, to pray continually would mean saying prayers uninterruptedly day and night. We need hardly attempt this to realize that it would not get us very far. If, on the other hand, prayer is simply communication with God, it can go on continually. In peak moments of awareness this communication will be more intense, of course. At other times it will be low key. But there is no reason why we should not be able to communicate with God in and through everything we do or suffer and so "pray without ceasing" (1 Thess 5:17).

Maybe I shouldn't have mentioned uninterrupted prayer at all. The very thought may seem overawing and scare someone off. Many of us might, in fact, say: "Praying at all times? Goodness! From where I find myself it would be a long way even to praying at those times when I am saying my prayers!" All right, then, let us start once again where we are. What is it that makes our prayers truly prayer? If only we could somehow catch on to the secret of that spontaneous prayerfulness. That would be the clue to praying when we are saying prayers. Eventually it may even lead to praying at all times.

Those of us who have been saying prayers every day for many years and who have been trying to make our prayers truly prayer should have some answer to the question: What is it that makes prayers prayer? When we try to put into words what the secret might be, words like mindfulness, full alertness, and wholehearted attention suggest themselves. Those are, of course, the characteristics also of our spontaneous moments of prayer. The difference is that the wakefulness which comes spontaneously at those special moments often costs us an effort at times of formal prayer. The technical term for that effort and for the state of mind that results from it is, in the Catholic tradition, "recollection."

Most Catholic Christians know what recollection means. At least they are familiar with the term. Others might associate recollection with memories. As a technical term, however, recollection means a special kind of mindfulness in prayer, a mindfulness that is identical with prayerfulness. When I am fully recollected, my prayers are fully prayer. As I get more and more distracted, my prayers run dry. Finally, my prayers may be an empty formality. When recollection is scattered by distractions, prayers are merely the empty husk of prayer. If recollection is that important for our prayer life, it might be worthwhile to examine more closely what we mean by it, and how we can cultivate that special kind of prayerful mindfulness.

Mindfulness implies concentration. Concentration is, therefore, an essential ingredient of recollection in prayer. Those of us who have learned to concentrate on what we are doing are well on the way to recollection. And yet, no amount of concentration will, by itself, make us recollected. The reason is this: Concentration normally narrows down our field of attention. It makes all our attentiveness converge on one focal point and, in the process, tries to eliminate everything else from our field of vision. We could compare this process of concentration with focusing a large magnifying glass. At first a good portion of the page might appear within its frame, but blurred. As we bring one single word or letter clearly into focus, all else is eliminated from our view. In a similar sense, concentration normally implies elimination.

Now, recollection is that full kind of mindfulness which T.S. Eliot calls "concentration without elimination." This is, of course, a paradox. But shouldn't we expect a paradox here? Do not all opposites coincide in God? How then could we encounter God in prayer and not be struck by paradox?

But how can there be a concentration *without* elimination? Because concentration can remain itself and yet coincide with an altogether different attitude that makes it include all that concentration alone would tend to eliminate. Recollection has two ingredients. Concentration is only one. The other one is what I call wonderment. For lack of a better term, wonderment stands here for a kind of sustained surprise. But our two ingredients of recollection do not mix easily. Wonderment and concentration seem to run counter to one another. While concentration tends to narrow down one field of vision, as we saw, wonderment is expansive. That these two movements coincide in recollection is just another expression of the paradox. Even the two bodily gestures associated with wonderment and concentration contradict one another. When we want to concentrate, we wince our eyes. We might think that this helps us focus our vision on something we want to look at with great concentration. But watch what happens when we want to concentrate intently on a faint or distant sound. We might also find ourselves wincing our eyes as we say, "I can barely make out what I'm hearing." Are we wincing our eyes so as to hear better? Well, we can't very well wince our ears, and yet our body wants to express the idea of eliminating everything except the one thing pinpointed for concentrated attention.

When you are filled with wonderment, however, your eyes are wide open. Just think of the eyes of a child in the zoo looking up to the elephants. Or think of your own eyes when you are standing under a starlit sky. You might even find yourself opening your arms wide as if your wide open eyes were not enough for your body to express your limitless openness.

Recollection combines this openness with concentration. How is my body to express this paradox? Am I going to wince one eye and open the other wide? I'm at a loss. But my heart can somehow deal with this paradox. That may be the reason why wholeheartedness comes closer to conveying the idea of recollection than mindfulness does. Paradox boggles the mind. But the heart thrives on paradox. We said that to speak of the heart is to speak of fullness. But only paradox can hold that fullness. The child in us understands this. For the child, too, thrives on paradox.

The little syllable "re" in recollection seems to imply the repetition of some previous activity, or the restoration of a previous condition. The word recollection suggests the process of re-establishing a collectedness which we once had and later lost. It suggests gathering together again the fragments of our original wholeness. "Oh, now I know why I have a hard time with recollection," someone might say. "How can I be re-collected when I've never been collected in the first place?" But no one has an excuse along this line of argument. At one time we have all been whole in this sense, full of wonderment and fully concentrated: when we were small children. That "becoming like children" which the Gospel demands as a condition for entering the Kingdom of Heaven is closely connected, then, with recollection, with cultivating the original wholeness of the child in us.

We need only watch little children in their playpen to realize how perfectly they combine concentration with wonderment. Often they are so concentrated on sucking the ear of a toy rabbit or simply on wiggling their toes that you might have a hard time trying to divert their attention to something else. If only our children could grow up without losing their power of recollectedness. How often adults destroy that gift with the best intentions. Children have a need to stand and look. A simple thing may absorb their attention for a long time. But then you see everywhere adults pulling children out of their wonderment and concentration. "Let's go. We have no time"—and a long arm pulls the poor child along. No wonder that so many marvelous children turn into dull adults. No wonder that their wholeness is scattered and their sense of mystery lost. "Don't just stand there; do something!" Well, healthier cultures had a different view of education. Some native American tribes would say, "A well-educated child ought to be able to sit and look when nothing is to be seen, to sit and listen when nothing is to be heard." Where this attitude prevails, children have a better chance to learn the art of tapping the Source of meaning, the art of prayer.

But even for us, it is never too late to recover that prayerfulness which is as natural to us as breathing. The child within us stays alive. And the child within us never loses the talent to look with the eyes of the heart, to combine concentration with wonderment, and so to pray without ceasing. The more we allow the child within us to come into its own, the more we become mature in our prayer life. This is surely one meaning of the saying that we must "become like children." There is no childishness suggested here. Jesus says to become not remain like children. We are not to be trapped by the child within us. But neither are we to be alienated from it. A truly mature person has not rejected childlikeness, but rather achieved it on a higher level. As we progress in that direction, everything in our daily life becomes prayer. The childlike heart divines springs of refreshing water at every turn.

But where shall we start? Once again, I can only suggest that we start where we are, that we begin with what comes easiest. Why not start by surveying a typical day? What is it you tend to tackle with spontaneous mindfulness, so that without an effort your whole heart is in it? Maybe it's that first cup of coffee in the morning, the way it warms you and wakes you up, or taking your dog for a walk, or giving a little child a piggyback ride. Your heart is in it, and so you find meaning in it—not a meaning you could spell out in words, but meaning in which you can rest. These are moments of intense prayerfulness, though we might never have thought of them as prayer. They show us the close connection between praying and playing. These moments when our heart finds ever so briefly rest in God are samples that give us a taste of what prayer is meant to be. If we could maintain this inner attitude, our whole life would become prayer.

Granted, it is not an easy task to maintain the mindfulness, gratefulness, prayerfulness we experience in those wholehearted moments. But at least we know now what we are aiming to maintain. It is like learning to balance a pencil on the tip of a finger. Talking about it is not much help. But when for once we have managed to do it, we know at least that we can do it, and how it is done. The rest is a matter of practice, of doing it over and over again, till it becomes second nature. Applied to prayer, this might mean eating and drinking every mouthful as mindfully as we drink that first cup of coffee. Soon we discover that eating and drinking can be prayer. Indeed, a meal ought to be a prayer. If we are to "pray without ceasing," how could we stop praying while we eat and drink?

This approach has yet another advantage. It allows us to speak about prayer without using religious jargon. If we said "prayer," someone might think we mean an activity to be added to our daily tasks. Right away we'd be back in the confusion between prayer and prayers. But if we call it mindfulness or wholehearted living, it is easier to recognize prayer as an attitude that should characterize all our activities. The more we come alive and awake, the more everything we do becomes prayer. Eventually, even our prayers will become prayer. Some people find it easier to eat and drink prayerfully—mindfully—than to say their prayers prayerfully. Should this surprise anyone? Why assume that our prayer life starts with saying prayers? If prayerfulness is our highest degree of aliveness, the starting point might be whenever we spontaneously come alive. Does it seem easier to recite a Psalm with recollection than to eat or drink or walk or hug with that same wonderment and concentration? It may well be the other way around. For some of us, saying prayers wholeheartedly may be the crowning achievement after we have learned to make every other activity prayer.

What matters is prayer, not prayers. But if this

is so, if prayerfulness is all that counts, who needs prayers? The answer is simple: everyone. Prayers fill a need we all experience, the need to express our prayerfulness. We cannot be mindful without being grateful. As soon as we awake from taking everything for granted, there is at least a glimmer of surprise and a beginning of gratitude. But gratitude needs to express itself. We know the awkward feeling we get from an anonymous gift. When I receive one, it is as if something were bottled up within me, and all morning I find myself expressing something like thanks to everyone I meet, just to satisfy my own need for doing so. But something else happens. As I express my gratitude, I become more deeply aware of it. And the greater my awareness, the greater my need to express it. What happens here is a spiraling ascent, a process of growth in ever expanding circles around a steady center, a movement leading ever more deeply into gratefulness.

And so with prayers. As the expression of our prayerfulness, prayers make us more prayerful. And that greater prayerfulness needs to express itself again in prayers. We might not have much to begin with, but the spiral expands according to its own inner dynamics, as long as we stay with it.

One image in which this dynamic movement of growth seems perfectly crystallized is the chambered nautilus. I can never pass a shell display without looking for one of these fascinating seashells. The specimens I find most exciting are the ones cut in half to show the whole suite of empty chambers with their pearly inner walls. Somewhere in the South Pacific or the Indian Ocean a mollusk built this marvelous shell around its body. And as this mysterious sea creature grew, it moved from chamber to chamber, scaling off the old one it had outgrown as it moved to a new and bigger one. But soon this new one too grew too small and forced its mason and inmate to build again and move on.

> Year after year beheld the silent toil
>   That spread his lustrous coil;
>   Still, as the spiral grew,
> He left the past year's dwelling for the new,
> Stole with soft step its shining archway through,
>   Built up its idle door,
> Stretch'd in his last-found home, and knew the old
>   no more.

These lines are from a poem by Oliver Wendell Holmes, "The Chambered Nautilus." The poet thanks our small soft shellfish, that "child of the wandering sea," for its message, still echoing through its chambers long after it left. A "heavenly message" the poet calls it, because it has to do with growing toward our ultimate goal. He says of that message:

> While on mine ear it rings,
> Through the deep caves of thought I hear a voice
>   that sings:—
>
>   Build

Build thee more stately mansions, O my soul,
  As the swift seasons roll!
  Leave thy low-vaulted past!
Let each new temple, nobler than the last,
Shut thee from heaven with a dome more vast,
  Till thou at length art free,
Leaving thine outgrown shell by life's unresting
  sea!

Once we realize how the interplay between prayerfulness and prayers builds the temple of our prayer life, we should be able to ask the right questions to see where we stand in this process and how we need to proceed. Our prayers have a twofold relationship to our prayerfulness, as we have seen. Prayers both express and reinforce our prayerfulness. Hence we need to ask two basic questions: Are my prayers a genuine expression of my prayerfulness? Do they make me more prayerful?

Since these two questions go to the heart of the matter, we can use them to check both prayers in community and prayers by ourselves. The context will be so different, however, that we shall here test these two areas one by one. Let us begin by looking into what are often called private prayers.

"Private prayers" is a misleading phrase. First of all, true prayers are never private. If prayers are private, they are not truly prayer. Whatever is private excludes someone. A private club has an exclusive membership; if a road is private, all but the owners are deprived of its use. But genuine prayer comes from the heart, from that realm of my being where I am one with all. It is never a private affair. Genuine prayer is all-inclusive. A great teacher of prayer in the Jewish tradition expressed this well: "When I prepare myself to say my prayers, I unite myself with all who are closer to God than I am, so that, through them, I may reach God. And I also unite myself with all who may be farther away from God than I am, so that, through me, they may reach God." Christian tradition calls this the communion of saints. Whenever we pray, we pray in community. This is why some prefer to speak of "personal" rather than "private" prayers. But that won't get us far. What is the alternative to personal prayer? Impersonal prayer? Let us hope that there is no such thing. Still, we do need to distinguish between praying together with others and praying by ourselves. I will call these two areas prayers together and prayers alone.

It helps to get rid of the term "private" when we speak of prayers. But retaining the term "prayers," we are still running the risk of misunderstanding. Let us make it clear that we do not necessarily mean set prayers out of a prayer book. Once more, we must distinguish prayer from prayers. Prayer, as we have seen, should go on without interruption. Through prayerfulness, *every* activity can and should become prayer. What we call prayers, on the other hand, is *one* activity among others—time out, as it were, for nothing but prayer. What we put into that time slot may be set prayers, but it may equally well be prayers in a wider sense. Our time set aside for prayers will be well spent if whatever we do in it gives expression to our prayerfulness and so makes us more prayerful.

There is only one basic rule for prayers alone: Make sure you are left alone. Once this is assured, it will be quite easy to find your own expression of whatever it is that fills your heart at that time. But being left alone in prayer is not as easy as one might think. Especially in religious communities, there are sometimes those whose religious observance consists largely in observing others. When and where and how you say prayers, for how long and in what posture—every detail is apt to come under scrutiny. It may be a great blessing to be able to discuss all these points with a teacher of prayer who will guide us to find what is most helpful for us personally. But beyond that, we have a right and a duty to insist: Concerning my prayers alone, leave me alone.

Yes, we have a duty in this respect. The most frequent interference does not come from the outside, but from within ourselves; it is not restricted to those who live in communities, but all of us have to struggle against it. There is within each one of us, I suspect, that little voice that will not leave us alone. It keeps urging us to conformity with some arbitrary model of prayer, or to non-conformity. In either case we get preoccupied with a model that we imitate or reject, instead of facing the challenge to be creative in our prayers alone. You are unique. If your prayer is genuine, it will be the grateful expression of your uniqueness.

This will be so, even if you don't make up your own prayers, but select from a book what suits you; the process of selecting will be creative and your choice will be unique. Leave me alone means: Leave me free to choose. Leave me free, if I so choose, not to use words at all, but silence, or dance, or music, or anything that expresses and nourishes my prayerfulness. It is as with food. There are thousands of different diets. What matters is that you find your own, the one that suits you and keeps you healthy.

This comparison introduces another aspect of prayers: discipline. Some people stay healthy on a vegetarian diet, others on meat; some eat only once a day, others eat several times. One discipline may be as healthy as another, but without discipline in food and drink no one can stay healthy for long. The same is true for discipline in prayer.

Discipline is one thing; however, regimentation is another. Discipline is the attitude of the disciple, the pupil who looks into the teacher's eye and is mirrored in the teacher's pupil. A drill sergeant couldn't care less about eye contact with the men in his regiment. Conformity is all that matters. But eye contact with the teacher encourages creative discipline and disciplined creativity in the pupils.

Regimentation is rigid and brittle. Discipline is as strong as it is flexible. Regimentation is lifeless, discipline alive and life-giving. When we pray alone, the great challenge is this: to free ourselves from regimentation (by others or by ourselves) and to look with the eyes of our heart at who we are in God's eyes, so that discipline may make us creative. There is no limit to creativity when we pray by ourselves.

What then of prayers together? When we pray with others, the one basic rule is: Do it together! That is a different thing from praying side by side. Sardines in a box are neatly side by side. But are they really together? The school of fish I'm watching from the pier moves spontaneously in different directions, but they are truly together as they share in one living space and one life. The ones in the box are dead. They know neither spontaneity nor sharing. When we get ready for prayers together, we might sometimes ask ourselves: Which of the two kinds of sardines do we resemble? (Remember, the side-by-side ones had to sacrifice their heads to fit so neatly into the box.)

Some people feel threatened when they hear talk about spontaneity in praying together. They think spontaneity is opposed to structure and so they are afraid to lose the support which structure gives them. But spontaneity goes with structure. Without structure there can be no spontaneity. Suppose you came to a party and the hostess told you, "We have prepared nothing, so as to allow for maximum spontaneity." It takes a great deal of preparation to make spontaneity possible. Of course, when the prepared structures get oppressive, they leave

no breathing space of spontaneity. For prayers together we need enough structure to support spontaneity, but no more. The trouble is that in a group
with great diversity some may feel stifled by structures which others find barely sufficient for support.
This will demand great care in preparing and great
patience on the part of all.

Similarly with sharing. We cannot pray together
without sharing. But sharing has many forms and
degrees. Taking part, taking your part, each one
taking his or her own part in praying together, that
is certainly basic and it surely is a form of sharing. In
fact, our prayers together could often be improved
if we let different people each take their share instead of doing everything in chorus together. (Invariably, singing in community can be improved by
letting only a small group sing the verses, and all
come in on the chorus. Yet, how rarely we avail
ourselves of these simple means to improve participation. After all, participation means taking part,
not taking the whole.) Sharing personal intentions
and concerns will be possible only when we know
the others well and feel comfortable with them.
Here, too, as with spontaneity, people in one and
the same group will find themselves on different
levels. We can only presume the lowest common
denominator of intimacy and start moving up from
there with great tact and patience.

Most of our problems with praying together
come from expecting too much. It would be unfair
to expect from a common kitchen food seasoned to

your own particular taste. We should not expect from praying together what we can only find when we pray alone. But there are advantages to a common kitchen. By praying with others, we find a support which most of us need and cannot get from praying alone. Through prayers by ourselves we express a prayerfulness in which we are alone; in order to celebrate the prayerful life we live in common, we have to pray together.

To light a candle by myself is one of my favorite prayers. I am not talking about reading prayers by candlelight. The very act of lighting the candle is prayer. There is the sound of striking the match, the whiff of smoke after blowing it out, the way the flame flares up and then sinks, almost goes out until a drop of melted wax gives it strength to grow to its proper size and to steady itself. All this and the darkness beyond my small circle of light is prayer. I enter into it as one enters a room. My being alone is essential to this prayer. The presence of even one other person would completely change it. Something would be lost.

To light a candle in a candlelight procession is an altogether different experience. Yet, this too can truly be prayer. At the Easter Vigil, the lighting of hundreds of candles from the one paschal candle can become a powerful lifting up of heart and mind to God for a whole community, and so a genuine prayer together. There is no way of repeating this prayer by oneself. This holds true of all prayers together, although it may not always be as obvious.

Can one ever experience by praying alone what is most distinctive about praying together?

But here, too, we need to ask ourselves, and now as a community, those two basic questions: Are our prayers together a genuine expression of the prayerfulness we share? Do they make us, as a community, more prayerful? Sometimes it happens that a community lives and works quite prayerfully together; the only part of their life that is not really prayerful are their prayers. One rushes, one drags; one sings flat, one sharp; one wants the window open, one wants it shut. They grind on each other, and when they finish their prayers, they need a few hours to recover their prayerfulness. In a case like that, let us take courage from the fact that we are united at least in wanting to pray together. But let us bravely tackle the problem how best to do it. By airing our two basic questions with patience and mutual trust, we may hope to get at the root of our difficulties and shall certainly find forms for our prayers together that will be genuine and rewarding.

After all, what counts are not our prayers but our prayer, not our prayerfulness but the forms by which we express and sustain it. How easily we slide into thinking of our prayers as the "real" prayer. What is the "real" prayer, the grace we say at the table or the meal that follows it? What could be more "real" than eating and drinking? And if we pray at all times, as we should, our eating and drinking will be real prayer. Rightly understood, our prayers at table will be an expression of thankfulness and a reminder to eat every bite of this meal thankfully. Gratefulness will turn the whole meal into prayer, for after we pray our prayers, we will pray our soup, salad, and dessert, and then pray another set prayer at the end as a reminder to continue to pray even after the meal.

As soon as we get the relationship of prayers to prayer confused, we begin to think that truly prayerful people can be recognized by longer and more frequent prayers. This would be like thinking that the best car is the one that uses the most fuel. In fact, a good case could be made for the claim that spiritual athletes get more mileage out of few prayers. It is not prayers that count, but prayerfulness.

To use a less crude imagery, we might think of prayers as the poetry of our prayer life. A poem celebrates life and in that celebration becomes itself a high point of life. We look with the eyes of our heart, are overawed by the wonders we see, and celebrate that vision by a gesture that taps the very source of life. But it can be said much more simply: Prayer is grateful living.

Contemplation and Leisure

Stonehenge, the mysterious monument in England, more than three and a half thousand years old, is a circular arrangement of enormous rock pillars. There are scores of them up to thirty feet in height and fifty tons in weight. No one knows by what ingenious means they were moved to this place from a quarry twenty miles away or how they were capped with huge slabs of rock for lintels. No one is even sure who accomplished this feat. Neither the ideas that bound them together nor the ideals that inspired their common effort are known to us. All is shrouded in the darkness of pre-history. We look at the intricate pattern of pillars, ditches, banks, and pits as we would look at runes inscribed on a rock. We cannot decipher their meaning. And yet we do find one clue. The plan of Stonehenge is clearly aligned to the point of sunrise at the summer solstice and to other points on the horizon where sun and moon rise on significant days of their cycles. The whole elaborate structure turns out to be a

giant walk-in sundial—and a moondial, too. Stonehenge translates the cycles of sun and moon into
architecture, movement into design, time into
space. This small part of earth is patterned on the
heavens. Order observed above gives rise to order
realized below. Here lies the key to the meaning of
Stonehenge. It is the key also to the meaning of
contemplation.

It often helps to follow the linguistic roots of a
word if we want to understand more deeply what it
means. The little syllable "temp" in our "con-temp-
lation" is of ancient origin. Scholars tell us that, in
the beginning, it might have meant something like
making a notch. You make a notch, and you have a
simple device for starting to count and to measure.
You can keep count of the fish you almost caught if
you mark each near-catch by a notch on the gun-
wale of your boat. Two notches a short distance
apart turn any stick into a measuring rod and allow
you to measure the fish that didn't get away.
Though far removed from its original meaning of
"notch," the syllable "temp" still has something to
do with measure today. Even in modern English
usage temperature is the measure of heat and cold,
temperament the measure of psychological response, tempo the measure of temporal rhythmic
recurrence. To temper means to adjust ingredients
in proper measure. If you have the virtue of temper-
ance, you eat and drink no more than is good for
you. You know your measure.

The word "temple" comes from the same root.

It is the word most directly related to contemplation, and it conjures up associations with the temple-
like structures at Stonehenge. Originally, however,
the Latin word for temple, *templum,* did not mean
an architectural structure, but stayed closer to the
sense of measure. It meant a measured area. That
measured area was not even on the ground but in
the sky. Only later did *templum* come to mean a
sacred precinct on the ground, corresponding to the
one in the sky, and finally the building erected in
that sacred space according to sacred measure-
ments.

It was the *templum* in the sense of a section of
the sky, however, which the Roman priests, the
augurs, contemplated. That means that they fixed
their gaze on it with sustained attention, and from
what they saw they deduced the most auspicious
course of action. In classical Rome, no important
public decision was made unless the proposed plan
agreed with what the augurs saw. This practice expresses a frame of mind older than logical reasoning,
an archetypal syndrome deeply ingrained in our
human psyche. We still have access to that depth
today, and by exploring it we can shed new light on
contemplation.

"Above" and "below" have a significance for us
humans which analytical thought cannot fathom.
Inevitably we speak with approval of "higher"
things. We call them elevated, exalted, above the
norm. In contrast, what is below our standards we

call inferior, lowly, base. It is subverting to our world view, not merely confusing to our language, if we speak of low-grade merchandise as precious and high accomplishment as failure. This must have something to do with the fact that we grow up, not down like carrots. Not even the clumsiest of us will fall up when we fall down. The consistency with which above and below polarize all human thought and language is surprising enough. That up vs. down implies everywhere the same value judgment (improvement vs. decline) is even more astounding. Even a revolutionary who strives to bring *down* what is currently on top does so out of the conviction that justice ought to prevail *over* injustice. Regardless of our philosophies and convictions, we all share a sense that there is something wrong when things are upside down.

It may be worth noting that it makes a difference for the meaning of "high" whether we contrast it with "low" or with "deep." High and deep may coincide sometimes; high and low never coincide. A high-minded person will think deep thoughts, but never low ones. In Latin *altus* means exalted in the sense of both high and deep (the high sea is deep), but the exalted is always in opposition to the base and lowly. It takes no more than common sense to appreciate these distinctions. Was Chesterton wrong in this regard when he pointed out that common sense is not so commonly found? The common sense that makes us understand relationships like those between high, deep and low must be older than language. It is closer to *sense* than to thought. And it seems to be *common* to all human beings.

This is solid ground. Let us make the most of it. Let us for a moment focus on the fact that the way in which we experience high and low puts a basic order into our human view of the word. The basic notion of order is simply implied in what I have called our common sense. That common sense tells us that order is to be valued higher than disorder, that there are degrees of order, and that we are able to rise to a higher level or order, somewhat in the way one scales a mountain, by facing up to the challenge, by measuring up to it. (We can scale down our ambitions, but once we accept a challenge, we have to measure up to it. Language does not even allow us to speak of measuring down; that would not make sense.)

This is the point at which contemplation comes in. To contemplate means raising our eyes to a higher order that challenges us to measure up. This is what the augurs meant to do. This is what Stonehenge tried to realize: to measure human life by a higher order and so to transform and perfect action through vision. Thirty-eight centuries ago humans like us stood there at Stonehenge under the deep dome of the night sky and understood something about human life for which the intellect alone is too shallow. Only the heart is high and deep enough to hold this vision. Only life lived to the full measures up to the task of contemplation.

Those who first introduced the term "contemplation" into our Christian vocabulary, in spite of the fact that it still was a technical term of the rival Roman religion, must have found it irreplaceable. They may well have been aware that contemplation stands for a primordial and universal human reality. They realized, for sure, that the concept was central to biblical tradition. It stands behind a whole theology of the temple, connecting Moses, the great contemplative, with Solomon's temple and with the temple that divine Wisdom builds; with Jesus Christ, in whom both Wisdom and the temple are seen personified; and with His Body, the new humankind, temple of the Holy Spirit.

For us, today, Moses is the great lawgiver, rather than the contemplative. But at a closer look he fits the contemplative model quite closely. He goes up to the mountain, to the higher realm; he exposes himself to the transforming vision, so much so that the afterglow of God's glory shines with blinding brightness on his face; and he brings down to the people not only the law, but the building plan for the temple. Again and again the Bible emphasizes that Moses built the tabernacle precisely according to the pattern that had been shown to him on the mountain. And even the law must be understood as a kind of plan according to which the people are to be built up into a temple of the living God. They become living stones rising to measure up to the vision of a divine order that must in the end shatter all measure.

Only by sustaining the tension between the ideal and its realization, between vision and action, may we hope to build the temple. And only by building the temple does contemplation prove that it is genuine. The little prefix "con-" (*cum*, with, together) should remind us that merely gazing at the vision is not contemplation at all. It might at best deserve to be called "templation." *Con*templation joins vision and action. It puts the vision into action. Action without vision is action running in circles, mere activism. Vision without action is barren vision. Throughout history, genuine contemplatives saw what needed to be done and what they saw to be necessary they simply did. That is why some of them had to work as tirelessly as Catherine of Siena, Bernard of Clairvaux, or Teresa of Avila. The temple on which they worked is still rising.

Bernard was so steeped in his inner vision that his outward eyes seemed blind at times. When the upper windows of his abbey church needed repair, the monks in charge asked him to make the decision. To their surprise Bernard did not know what they were talking about. In all those years, the abbot had never looked around in church, we are told. He had never noticed that there were any upper windows. But when it came to shaping Europe according to the light of his inner vision, Bernard, the last of the Fathers, became the first international diplomat of an emerging Christian West.

Or take Catherine of Siena. Still in her teens, she set out on a vision quest, like the youths of some

Native American tribes. For years she stayed in seclusion, intent on nothing but the inner vision. She buried herself in obscurity. As her father's twenty-third child, alone in a back room of his house, she was well hidden. Yet, a decade later she stands in the limelight of history. An ambassador for peace, this laywoman, not yet thirty, persuades the Pope to return from Avignon to Rome. The great mystic rises to the challenge of her vision and becomes a great woman of action.

Teresa of Avila's life shows us that this matching of vision by action means more than putting theory into practice within. There is her vision of watering the soul's garden, of journeying from mansion to mansion to the luminous center of the Interior Castle. And outwardly there is her entanglement in Church politics, in fighting, and intrigue. The two seem worlds apart, at first sight. She was not shown a blueprint for reforming the Carmelites, ready to be carried out. That is not how contemplation works. She simply exposed her heart to the radiance of "the temple not built by human hands." And in its light it became clear to her, step by step, where the building of the temple here below needed a helping hand. That she was obedient to that vision was what made her the great contemplative.

What is it that makes it so difficult for us to hold vision and action together in contemplation? Maybe it is this: each half of the double challenge of contemplation seems by itself more than enough for our strength. Putting vision and action together seems asking too much. How tiresome merely to do the same round of chores again and again, faithful to detail, careful to avoid mistakes, patient when they invariably happen. And how strenuous to keep the inner eye focused on the light. But as long as I take these two efforts separately, I remain in control. As I pay attention, now to the vision, now to the action, it is I who determine the price. I pay what I consider fair and go no further. But when I put vision and action together, the task becomes demanding. *It* demands. I can no longer set the price. When we speak of a demanding task, we mean more than strenuous action. The action can only make me tired. But the vision, if I dare face it, might demand that I go on, in spite of being tired. The little "con" which puts vision and action together is what makes *con*templation demanding and, therefore, so difficult.

And yet, if we allowed this contemplative tension between action and vision to snap, meaning would fade out of any purpose we pursue. For what I have called action and vision might just as well be called purpose and meaning. You may have been engaged in pursuing a purpose for a long time, when suddenly you wake up to the question: What is the meaning of it all? Meaningless purpose is mere drudgery. Yet, the meaning you find in what you do will inevitably challenge you. It will make you responsible. You are no longer running in circles, but this new-found sense of direction makes new demands on you. To see a little more clearly what life

is all about makes it more exciting, more worthwhile, but by no means easier. That may be the
reason why there is something within us that would
rather settle for drudgery than rise to the challenge
of responsibility to go beyond ourselves.

In sloppy everyday speech we sometimes use
purpose and meaning interchangeably as if they
meant the same. But remember how we go about a
given purpose and how, in contrast, we experience
meaning. The difference is striking. In order to
achieve our purpose, whatever it may be, we must
take hold of the situation, take matters in hand, take
charge of things. We must be in control. Is this also
true of a situation in which you experience deep
meaning? You will find yourself saying that you
were touched, moved, even carried away by the
experience. That doesn't sound as if you were in
control of what happened. Rather, you gave yourself
to the experience, it took hold of you and so you
found meaning in it. Unless you take control, you
won't achieve your purpose; but unless you give
yourself, you can't experience meaning.

There is a tension between this giving and taking. It is the tension between meaning and purpose,
between vision and action. If we let this tension
snap, our life becomes polarized. But to maintain
creative tension is demanding. It demands from us a
self-giving we find difficult. Why difficult? Because
it demands courage. As long as we are in control, we
feel safe. But when we allow ourselves to be carried
away, there is no telling where things will lead. All

we know is that life gets adventuresome. But there is risk implied in adventure. Sometimes that risk frightens us so much that we'd rather keep things tightly under control, even though this means settling for boredom.

Do you remember how this works in personal relationships? You think you are safe with someone: "I know how to handle him," or "I've got her number." But if you keep a relationship too tightly under control, it soon gets boring. So you open up a little. Right away it gets adventuresome, but risky, too. You never know what will happen next when you begin to give yourself to that adventure. When you get scared enough, you quickly clam up again. Sometimes we keep going back and forth between giving and taking back, opening ourselves and clamming up, many times a day.

But life is give-and-take, not give or take. Spasmodic gasping is one thing, healthy breathing another. When we take a hearty breath, we give ourselves to the air we inhale; and when we give it out again, we take a quick break from breathing. This balance of giving and taking is a key to healthy living on every level of life. In fact, balance is too mechanical a word to apply to the intimate intricacy of this give-and-take. We are talking about a giving within taking and a taking within giving. Once this is spelled out, it is hardly necessary to stress the fact that we are not playing off giving against taking. By no means. We are playing off a life-giving give-and-take against a mere taking that is as deadly as a mere giving. It matters little whether you merely take a breath and stop, or give a breath and stop there. In either case, you're dead.

Most of us need a good deal of encouragement for giving. The way we are built (or, rather, forced into a warped shape by our society) the taking takes care of itself. It might be a good test if you checked for half an hour how often you say "I take" and how often "I give." The language we use gives us away. I take a course, take an exam, take a vacation, take a room, take a car, take a ride, take a trip, take a left, take a right, take a rest, take a walk, take a swim, take a drink, take a meal, and finally, when I'm worn out by all that taking, I take a nap. Or at least I try to take a nap, until I find out that I will hardly fall asleep until I give myself to that nap and let the nap take me. But some of us are so set on taking, so unable to give ourselves that we must knock ourselves out with sleeping pills before that poor nap gets a chance to take us.

This brings us to the topic of leisure. To recover a healthy understanding of leisure is to come a long way toward understanding contemplation. But few words we use are as misunderstood as the word "leisure." This shows itself right away when we speak of work and leisure as a pair of opposites. Are the two poles of activity really work and leisure? If this were so, how could we speak of leisurely work? It would be a blatant contradiction. We know, however, that working leisurely is no contradiction at all. In fact, work ought to be done with leisure, if it is to be done well.

What then is the opposite of work? It is play. These are the two poles of all activity: work and play. And what we have come to understand about purpose and meaning will help us see this more clearly. Whenever you work, you work for some purpose. If it weren't for that purpose, you'd have better things to do than work. Work and purpose are so closely connected that your work comes to an end, once your purpose is achieved. Or how are you going to continue fixing your car once it is fixed? This may be less obvious when you are sweeping the floor. Can't you go on sweeping even when there is not a speck of dust left? Well, you can go on making sweeping movements with your broom, but your purpose was accomplished, and so the work, as work, is ended. Sooner or later, someone is sure to ask you why you are playing around with that broom. What was work with purpose has now become play.

In play, all the emphasis falls on the meaning of your activity. If you tell your friends that you find it very meaningful to dance around with your broom on a Friday night, they might raise their eyebrows, but they cannot seriously object. Play needs no purpose. That is why play can go on and on as long as players find it meaningful. After all, we do not dance in order to get somewhere. We dance around and around. A piece of music doesn't come to an end when its purpose is accomplished. It has no purpose, strictly speaking. It is the playful unfolding of a meaning that is there in each of its movements, in every theme, every passage: a celebration of meaning. Pachelbel's Canon is one of the magnificent superfluities of life. Every time I listen to it, I realize anew that some of the most superfluous things are the most important for us because they give meaning to our human life.

We need this kind of experience to correct our world view. Too easily are we inclined to imagine that God created this world for a purpose. We are so caught up in purpose that we would feel more comfortable if God shared our preoccupation with work. But God plays. The birds in a single tree are sufficient proof that God did not set out with a divine no-nonsense attitude to make a creature that would perfectly achieve the purpose of a bird. What could that purpose be? I wonder. There are titmice, juncos, and chickadees; woodpeckers, gold finches, starlings and crows. The only bird God never created is the no-nonsense bird. As we open our eyes and hearts to God's creation, we quickly perceive that God is a playful God, a God of leisure.

But let us be careful not to fall into opposing leisure and work. Leisure is the balance of work and play. Leisure gives full measure to both. Yet even this could be misunderstood. Too quickly someone might say, "Yes, when I play, I have a good time; and when I work, let's get it over with; a perfect balance, isn't it?" Not all that perfect, it seems to me. Should I not also have a good time while I'm working? People who spend their working hours with no mind for anything but purpose are unlikely to begin playing when their free time finally comes. Either they will collapse and slump in a chair with a glass in their hand, for that kind of work wears one out completely. Or they will be so set in the groove of mere purpose that they will continue to work. Unable to play, they will either work overtime, or if they pick up their golf clubs or tennis racquets, they will give themselves a *work*out. We are simply unable to play playfully unless we learn to work playfully.

To work playfully! Doesn't that sound almost frivolous, given the attitude toward work that was drilled into many of us? Working playfully sounds to us like fiddling around. And yet the most efficient work is work done leisurely. And working leisurely means putting into our work what is most typical of play, namely the emphasis on meaning. Leisure gives meaning to purpose, makes room for meaning in the midst of purposeful activity. The Chinese character for leisure is made up of two elements that by themselves mean open space and sunshine: the attitude of leisure creates an opening to let the sun shine in. One late morning I saw a shaft of sunlight fall at a steep angle into the man-made canyon of Wall Street and understood what that ancient Chinese ideogram for leisure could mean for busy New Yorkers.

When our purposeful work also is meaningful,

we will have a good time in the midst of it. Then we will not be so eager to get it over with. If you spend only minutes a day getting this or that over with, you may be squandering days, weeks, years in the course of a lifetime. Meaningless work is a form of killing time. But leisure makes time come alive. The Chinese character for being busy is also made up of two elements: heart and killing. A timely warning. Our very heartbeat is healthy only when it is leisurely.

The heart is a leisurely muscle. It differs from all other muscles. How many push-ups can you make before the muscles in your arms and stomach get so tired that you have to stop? But your heart muscle goes on working for as long as you live. It does not get tired, because there is a phase of rest built into every single heartbeat. Our physical heart works leisurely. And when we speak of the heart in a wider sense, the idea that life-giving leisure lies at the very center is implied. Never to lose sight of that central place of leisure in our life would keep us youthful.

Seen in this light, leisure is not a privilege but a virtue. Leisure is not the privilege of a few who can afford to take time, but the virtue of all who are willing to give time to what takes time—to give as much time as a task rightly takes. With this we have come full circle and are back at contemplation. Only by looking up to the stars are we able to see the meaning of our purpose; only by putting our shoulder to the wheel are we able to translate the de-

mands of our vision into action. By calling this attitude leisure, we refer to its two poles as work and
play. When we refer to the same polarity in terms of
action and vision, we speak of contemplation. Call it
contemplation or call it leisure, the heightened
aliveness we mean springs from the creative tension
between purpose and meaning.

Contemplation		Leisure		
	(ideal)		(give)	
Vision	(order)	*Meaning*	(yourself)	Play
	(practical)		(take)	
Action	(realization)	*Purpose*	(in hand)	Work

As we recover this comprehensive sense of the
term contemplation, we are restoring a key term of
Christian spirituality to its full significance. But we
are doing much more. We are rescuing contemplation from specialists and returning it to all those to
whom it belongs as their birthright, to every human
being.

Far too long has contemplation been regarded
as the private domain of contemplatives. Contemplatives in this impoverished sense were only those
who were preoccupied with the vision of meaning
and withdrew from purpose and action. They often
set an example for the intensity with which we must
attune ourselves to the meaning of life, for the courage we need to expose ourselves to the demands of
our heart's vision. Yet only the greatest among them

have become examples of the dedication necessary to translate this vision into action. Maybe it is too much to expect excellence in both respects from any but the greatest among us. But all of us must strive to cultivate both, or else we grow lopsided. Only by cultivating a contemplative attitude can we become harmonious human beings. How, then, could we leave contemplation to the contemplatives? We must not allow the fancy word "contemplation" to frighten us. If it means life in the creative tension of purpose and meaning, who could escape its challenge? As we rise to that challenge of contemplation, we begin to discover the fullness of life for which our human heart longs.

Each of the previous chapters of this book dealt with a particular aspect of the contemplative tension. As we glance back at them from the vantage point we have reached, our key terms fall into place.

Prayerfulness		**Gratefulness**
	(looking with)	
Wonderment	(the heart)	*Heart-vision:* All is gratuitous
	(centering in)	
Concentration	(the heart)	*Heart-action:* Total response

When we spoke of the prayerfulness that makes our whole life prayer, we found that it implies concentration and wonderment. Looking back now, we become aware that these two components of prayerful recollectedness point in two directions:

toward purpose and toward meaning. There can be no purposeful action without concentration, and wonderment stands precisely for that wide vision that sees things related to their horizon of meaning.

To look with wonderment means looking with the eyes of the heart. And concentration in prayer is a centering in the heart. The heart is central in every respect. In our perspective, the heart connects prayerfulness and gratefulness, for the fullness of these two is the fullness the heart stands for. Heart vision perceives with surprise that the whole world and all we find within it is ultimately gratuitous. We live in a "given" world. To this gift character of all there is the heart gives its full response in thanks and praise and blessing.

Blessing, too, is an aspect of gratefulness. But what we mean by blessing is less clear than what we mean by thanks and praise. In my own struggle to understand blessing correctly, I came up against two difficult questions. The first one puzzled me in my early school days; with the second one I am still grappling.

At school we would sing songs like "Praise God From Whom All Blessings Flow." I had no problems with that. God was somehow high above us and blessing was flowing down on us like sunlight or spring rain. But then I stumbled onto verses like "Bless the Lord, O my soul" and "Wild beasts and tame, O bless the Lord!" This seemed upside down. Was I to bless God? Were not all blessings flowing from God? Were even tigers and poodles invited to do what I thought only God could do—bless!

I must have carried this question around with me for some time. But one day the answer literally popped out of the ground. It was on my way home from school one afternoon in early spring. The sun had licked up all the snow on the country road. All chances of catching a ride home by jumping a horse sleigh were gone, so we took the shortcut along the brook, testing the thin ice in spots as we ambled along. If ever one feels what a blessing warm sunshine can be, it is after a long winter in the Austrian Alps. Every foot of ground seemed to feel that blessing. And there, stomping through a soggy bottom, suddenly we children stood before the first flowers. Hundreds of coltsfoot blossoms were pushing through dead leaves. The whole bank was golden yellow.

Coltsfoot gets its name from the shape of its leaves, resembling a hoof print. But there were no leaves as yet, only the blossoms, more and more of them as we ran and looked. This was spring. Oh yes, there had been hellebores even in mid-winter. Christmas roses, we called them. When, on a sunny day between snowstorms, dry patches appeared on the southern slopes, we'd look and find them right under the snow, moon-white blooms. Sometimes one was tinged with light green or with a rosy flush like a cloud at dawn. Those winter roses, five pale petals and a tiny crown at the center, were stars from a world without seasons. But this was spring now. And these golden suns, no bigger than a nickel, each on its own sturdy stem, were the blessing earth sent up in answer to the blessing coming down from the sun. No other flower of the year, not even the huge sunflowers in September, would ever resemble the sun more closely than these very first blessings of spring.

There was my answer. No need to reason it out. I simply walked into it, saw it, became it, as my eyes blessed God and I knew what that meant. Blessing echoes blessing. That is the deep meaning of contemplation. The notion of blessing connects the temple above and the temple below. Our heart's most comprehensive vision shows us that all is gift—blessing. And, in response, our heart's most spontaneous action is thanksgiving—blessing.

But here my second question arises. What if I cannot recognize the given as a blessing? What if it is not sunshine that pours down on us, but hailstones like hammer-blows? What if it is acid rain? Here, again, the gift within the gift is opportunity. I have the opportunity, for example, to do something about that acid rain, face the facts, inform myself about the causes, go to their roots, alert others, band together with them for self-help, for protest. By taking each opportunity as it is offered, I show myself grateful. But my response will not be full unless I respond also to the ever-present opportunity to praise.

W.H. Auden has helped me see this by his poem

"Precious Five," especially by its last stanza. "I could," says Auden there,

> Find reasons fast enough
> To face the sky and roar
> In anger and despair
> At what is going on,
> Demanding that it name
> Whoever is to blame:
> The sky would only wait
> Till all my breath was gone
> And then reiterate
> As if I wasn't there
> That singular command
> I do not understand,
> *Bless what there is for being,*
> Which has to be obeyed, for
> What else am I made for,
> Agreeing or disagreeing?

To bless whatever there is, and for no other reason but simply because it is—that is our raison d'être; that is what we are made for as human beings. This singular command is engraved in our heart. Whether we understand this or not matters little. Whether we agree or disagree makes no difference. And in our heart of hearts we know it.

No matter how hard you strike a bell, it will ring. What else is it made for? Even under the hammer blows of fate the heart rings true. The human heart is made for universal praise. As long as we pick and choose, making praise depend on our approval, we are not yet responding from the heart. When we find our heart, we find that core of our being that is attuned to reality. And reality is praise-worthy. With clear vision the heart sees the ultimate meaning of all: blessing. And with clear intent the heart responds with the ultimate purpose of life: blessing.

"Praising, that's it," Rilke exclaims, in his *Sonnets to Orpheus.* And he presents Orpheus, the prototype of the poet, the human being at its most divine, as "one appointed to praise." "As one appointed to praise/he came forth like one from the stone's/silence." The image suggests bell-metal. In a different image, his heart is a wine press. The grapes are trod at one passing season. The wine, however, lasts. Not even the mold in the tombs of kings gives the lie to his song of praise. His is a message that lasts. And far into the doors of the dead he holds bowls with offerings, fruit of praise.

Of the human heart Rilke says in his *Duino Elegies:*

> Between hammers endures
> Our heart, as the tongue
> endures between teeth
> and still remains praising.

Thanksgiving, blessing, praise, all three belong to gratefulness. Each has its shortcomings. Praise may sound too formal for everyday living. Many may find the sound of blessing too churchly to feel at ease. Thanksgiving, in turn, tends to suggest a polite convention rather than the universal attitude toward life which we mean here. But each of the three terms adds to gratefulness an aspect that the other two fail to emphasize. Praise stresses a value-response. Blessing resonates with religious undertones. Thanksgiving implies deep personal engagement. All three together make gratefulness full.

Suddenly everything is simple. We can drop all the big, cumbersome terms. Gratefulness says it all. And gratefulness is something all of us know from experience. Can the spiritual life be that simple? Yes, what we secretly hoped is true: it is all that simple. It is this very simplicity, in fact, that we find most difficult. But why not drop the complications we put in our own way? What brings fulfillment is gratefulness, the simple response of our heart to this given life in all its fullness.

Faith and Beliefs

Faith: Trust in the Giver

Suppose our argument thus far is convincing. Suppose we agree that gratefulness is that fullness of life for which all of us are thirsting. Then the task ahead is simple enough: to learn to live gratefully. The key question is: How shall we go about it?

Earlier on, when we spoke of learning to live prayerfully, I suggested that we take the most prayerful moments in our daily life and start from there. This gives us the advantage of starting with something we already know from experience. In certain situations we have experienced an inner attitude that we consider prayerful; now the task is to approach not only some but all situations in that attitude. At least we already know what it is that we want to make our own in a more sustained way; we know it from the inside. That makes all the difference. We can never learn prayerfulness by mere imitation from the outside.

In learning gratefulness, we follow the same

84

pattern. We have experienced moments of gratefulness, and, therefore, we know from within the attitude we want to repeat and maintain. Those moments of deep gratefulness are, in fact, our moments of true prayerfulness, moments in which our heart is wide awake. We have already explored this and have come to recognize that prayer and thanks spring from the same root, from the heart. It is to those peak experiences of the heart that we must go back if we want to learn to live gratefully.

But wait—I have used an expression that might all too easily be misunderstood. What does it mean to go back to an experience? There are two ways of going back. One makes us draw new strength from the past; the other makes us shrivel up. What makes the difference? Let's put it this way. If I recall a past experience in order to clutch it and suck the last drop of sweetness from it greedily, it will yield nothing but disappointment. If, on the other hand, I recall the same experience merely to celebrate it, merely to single it out, to hold it up, to marvel at it once again, it will nourish me again and again. This is how I suggest that we recall the moments in which our heart was wakefully alive.

All we know about "life in fullness" flows from memories of that kind. All that we know about God by experience was given to us in those moments. And is there any kind of religious knowledge worth its name? When religious traditions speak of the divine life within us, they refer, implicitly at least, to our high points of wakeful awareness, to our mystical experiences. Yes, let us not shy away from that thought. We are all mystics. If mysticism is, by definition, the experience of communion with the Ultimately Real (God, if you feel comfortable with the term), then who can disclaim being a mystic? Unless we all had experiences of this kind, we wouldn't even know what we mean by rock-bottom Reality. We wouldn't even know, as we have seen, what "is" means, or "now." But we do know.

Just as we cannot leave contemplation to contemplatives, we cannot leave mysticism to mystics. It would mean cutting off the roots of human life. By putting mystics on a pedestal in our mind, high, out of reach, we don't do justice to them, nor to ourselves either. Paraphrasing what Ruskin said about being an artist, we could say: A mystic is not a special kind of human being; rather, every human being is a special kind of mystic. I might just as well rise to this challenge and become that unique, irreplaceable mystic that only I can become. There never was and never will be anyone exactly like me. If I fail to experience God in my own unique way, that experience will forever remain in the shadow land of possibility. But if I do, I will know life by the divine life within me.

My own tradition has much to say about that life-breath of God within us; Christian tradition speaks about God's presence in our hearts under three headings: Faith, Hope, and Love. These terms point to different aspects of one and the same living reality. But remember—we are dealing here with life. Life cannot be neatly sliced and packaged and remain alive. Faith, Hope, and Love are not three boxes, with specified contents, as it were. Rather they are ways of being alive, aspects of the one fullness of life that is our topic.

High peaks of aliveness are also always marked by intense gratefulness. Even people whose world view does not include a divine Giver to whom their thanks can be directed often experience deep gratitude in those moments. They experience it no less strongly than others, even though their own gratefulness gets mailed without an address, so to say. In any case, we know from experience that whenever we are truly awake and alive, we are also truly grateful. If, then, we want to go back (in the right way) to our peaks of wakefulness to learn gratefulness, a map of some kind would come in handy.

It is true that maps can never replace the experience of an explorer, but they do help even the most independent among us. Faith, Hope, and Love provide us with something like points on a map as we go back to our moments of grateful aliveness. In fact, these points of reference do more than lead us back to an experience; they also point forward toward putting Faith, Hope, and Love into daily practice. But Faith, Hope, and Love, rightly understood, are three aspects of gratefulness.

This use of reference points has another advantage. The map helps us to return to the territory of an actual experience, but in turn exploration of that territory helps us to update and correct our map. No matter how helpful maps are, they remain subject to correction through discoveries made by those who use them in their exploration. Spiritual maps are no exception in this regard. Those of us who know or think we know what our reference points signify may find to our surprise that Faith, Hope, and Love acquire new meaning in the process of being compared with data taken from our own experiences of overwhelming gratefulness.

Precisely those of us who are familiar with, say, the concept of faith might, in fact, be the first ones to wonder. Faith? What could my faith have to do with that moment on the mountain top (or in the midst of a traffic jam) when suddenly, for no obvious reason at all, everything makes sense? One reason for not seeing the connection could be that we never looked for something as obviously religious as faith anywhere else but in a setting clearly labeled "religious." Yet, labels tend to deceive. Do we know what "religious" means except through our own peak moments? In a full sense of knowing, we know nothing but what we have actually experienced. Faith is not first and foremost a collection of religious beliefs handed on to us by tradition. It has far more to do with that courageous trust in life that we know from our moments of inner breakthrough. It may come as a surprise, but authentic Christian tradition bears witness to precisely this meaning of faith.

In the Gospels, Scripture scholars tell us that there is not a single passage in which the Greek word for "faith" (*tietis*) means, strictly speaking, "beliefs." For example, that Jesus marveled at the Roman official's "faith" means that he was surprised by the man's deep trust, not by the way he could rattle off a list of beliefs. He would have found it hard to do so. And when Jesus reproved the disciples for their "lack of faith," he meant their lack of trust and courage; it wasn't a reprimand for dropping one or another article of faith from the creed. The reason is obvious: no creed existed. No beliefs had been spelled out. Faith was courageous trust in Jesus and in the good news which he lived and preached. Eventually, this trust would crystallize into explicit beliefs, it is true. But the starting point is trusting courage, not beliefs. And in our life of faith—just as in lighting a fuse—it makes a vital difference at which end we start.

Starting points are of great significance in the Bible. The first verse, the first image, the beginning of a story—these are often of prime importance for getting the point across. We ought to be alert to this fact in our Bible reading. What, for instance, is the very beginning of the story of our faith, as the Bible tells it? It starts with Abraham, whom we call "our Father in Faith." If faith consisted first and foremost in believing something, God would certainly start Abraham off by giving him a set of beliefs. But this is not so. Yes, God does give Abraham promises in which to believe, but first of all God challenges his trust. The beginning of faith is practically empty of content. It is pure trust.

"Go forth!" is God's first word to Abraham, the first verse of Chapter 12 of Genesis. "Go out!" is the challenge. "Venture forth!" The English language hardly lends itself to expressing the full impact of that calling. "Outgoing go out" comes closer to the original Hebrew. And then expression is piled on expression to make this venture as challenging as possible to Abraham's courage: "Go forth out of your land, and out of your kinsfolk, and out of your father's house." And where is he to go? ". . . into a land which I shall point out to you." Neither map, nor direction, nor name of destination was given to Abraham. It is as if God were saying to him: "Trust Me! I'll get you there. All you need is the courage to step out and leave everything behind." This is how Abraham becomes our Father in Faith. And, almost as a little aside, we are told at this point how old Abraham was when he ventured forth in faith: seventy-five! That's not exactly the age at which people feel most venturesome. It must have cost Abraham a fair amount of trust and courage.

There is another decisive beginning in the biblical history of faith, the starting point of God's covenant with Abraham. This time the account starts by telling us that Abraham was now ninety-nine years old. Since one hundred stands for perfection, we are alerted here that our Father in Faith is still not quite perfect. So God appears to Abraham and says, "I am El Shaddai" (Gen 17:1). That means, according to one way of reading that Hebrew name of God: I am the One who sets the limit; who tells you what "enough" means, who determines the measure of fullness and perfection. And what is it that Abraham is still lacking? "Walk in My sight and be perfect." This is what makes for perfection of faith: to walk in God's presence.

What does that mean? God is not saying: "Walk in My sight and pull yourself together, for I'm keeping a close eye on you!" Rather, that walking in God's sight is by itself a going toward perfection, step by step. This is, of course, something we come to understand only by doing it. But talking about it, as we are doing here, might help us at least to see more clearly what walking in God's sight demands from us. It demands no less than perfect trust and courage, perfect faith. Since this is not obvious at first sight, let's take a closer look at it (*give* ourselves to a closer look, I should say).

Before biblical passages can help us, we must allow them to put us on the spot. I must tell myself: Stop and listen! This concerns *you!* If this were merely a call addressed to Abraham, I'd be off the hook. But this means *me!* To face this fact calls for courage—the courage to accept myself, to accept myself as the person I am. Ah, how much easier this would be, I'm inclined to think, if I were Abraham, or at least St. Francis, or St. Teresa, or some other spiritual giant I admire—but little old me?

I so enjoy the story about the rabbi who prayed: "Lord, make me like Abraham!" Maybe he had been inspired by this very passage. "Gladly I would walk in Your presence," he prays, "but first, please make me like Abraham!" At this, a voice comes from heaven, saying: "Look, I've already got one Abraham!"

God has already got one of each of my admired models. The one whom God is calling here and now is no one else but me. No one but me has ever walked in God's sight with exactly the same background, the same talents, the same shortcomings. Yes, even our shortcomings seem to challenge God. Walk before Me, God says, and I will show you that I can lead even as unlikely a candidate as you to perfection. I can accept this offer only if I have the courage to accept myself. And that means accepting the way I am as a given reality—as given material to work with, as very much in need of change, maybe, but in any case given. In this way to accept myself as given is in itself a form of gratefulness.

But the challenge to be myself is only one implication of God's call to perfect faith. There is more to it. I must walk in God's sight, and it cannot be done by proxy. I look at myself and wish that I could at least dress up for the occasion, even if it were no more than Adam's little apron of fig leaves. I cannot beat the thought of naked exposure to God's sight. I hide, as Adam hid in the greenery. But there is God's voice calling me: "Adam, where are you?" This is God's challenge to expose myself in trust and courage. This second implication of the call to perfect faith seems far more demanding even than the challenge to be myself.

The challenge to expose myself, face to face, to God's sight is a double challenge. God calls and

Adam hears that call as: "Where are *you?*" Cain hears the same call as: "Where is your *brother?*" One single summons to come into God's presence calls for two different ways of doing so, depending on where we find ourselves. For Adam it means the challenge to face God by facing himself; for Cain it means facing God in his brother. These are two inseparable aspects of one and the same call. If I close my ears to one of them, my response to the other will be distorted.

The trouble is that we are apt to be off balance. Some of us are inclined to seek God exclusively in the secret recesses of our inner life, others exclusively in the encounter with people. Those of the first kind are never at a loss when God asks, "Where are *you?*" "Here I am, Lord. I have just examined my conscience and know exactly where I am. I'm not in danger of losing sight of myself. I don't allow others to distract me from the business of self-improvement." But God asks: "And where is your brother?"

Ah, now the others are getting their chance. They have their answer ready. "Which of my brothers would you like to know about, Lord? I have detailed information on every one of them. My sisters, too, in case you are interested. I keep close tabs on everyone. Here is my file box." But God asks: "And where are *you?*"—"Me? Oh, ah, I guess there is a card missing in my files!"

It sounds funny, as long as I allow myself to think of those two types as being out there somewhere. But when I realize that I have them both within myself, it gets less amusing. Yes, I find that I am apt to do the opposite of what a given moment calls for. Every time I hear the question "Where are you?" I seem to be busy with the affairs of others; and when I'm asked "Where is your brother?" I'm steeped in preoccupation with myself. And yet, if I am serious about exposing myself to God's presence like Abraham, our Father in Faith, I must rise up in trust and courage to face God both in myself and in others. Two different gestures, but one single response of faith.

There is a third challenge implied in God's call to Abraham. "Walk in My sight and (so) be perfect." This is addressed to me personally, and so it is a challenge to be myself. It summons me into God's presence, and so it is a challenge to expose myself to that presence in others and in my own heart. But this call is clearly also a challenge to *walk*. After all, we might have expected God to say "stand," or "kneel," or "fall down before Me." No, "walk" is the word. Walking demands more trust, more courage. Faith walks. Walking implies risk. And faith thrives on risk.

Throughout most of our lifetime, except occasionally, when there is sleet on the sidewalk, we are likely to forget that walking is risky business. But senior citizens know better—and toddlers, too. It's an awe-inspiring moment when that little quadruped in diapers rises up to stand for the first time on two legs. She wobbles, I admit, but she stands. And her face shows clearly that she's aware of the exciting risk she's taking. Then she lifts up one of those pudgy legs and—whoops, she's lost her balance. Later on we are no longer aware that we indeed do lose our balance with every step. We quickly regain it again. Yet, unless we took the risk of falling, we couldn't make one single step. And this is the form of locomotion God demands from us on the path of faith: not riding, not swimming, not flying, but walking—a constant losing and finding of our balance.

If we are afraid of making fools of ourselves, too proud to lose our balance even for a moment, too eager to cut a good figure in God's sight, we end up standing there like statues in dignified poses and make fools of ourselves, after all. But readiness to lose our balance is not enough. If, in the process, we stumble all over ourselves, it is just as foolish. We must dare to lose our balance, and yet keep it. We must dare to make fools of ourselves but be careful not to do it foolishly. Faith is the art of making fools of ourselves wisely like dancers.

At our peak moments of gratefulness, we find the threefold courage of faith easy. It comes quite naturally, because at those moments we respond to the challenge of life from our heart. When I find my heart, I also find the courage to be myself, for the heart stands for my very self. This true self is both unique and all-embracing. And so, when I find my heart, I also find the courage to expose myself, for the heart stands for the very point of encounter with self, with others, with God. God sees the heart and only with the eyes of the heart can I see God.

But when I find my heart, I also find the courage to walk, for the heart is my true center of gravity. The wise foolishness that springs from the heart is a dancer's graceful playfulness.

That primordial courage of our heart, as we know it in moments of wholehearted gratefulness, comes as close to perfect faith, in the biblical sense, as we might hope for. But it is one thing to experience that faith in a flash of enthusiasm, and quite a different thing to keep our courage seaworthy amidst the ups and downs of daily living. This is where our religious beliefs come in. They are meant to keep our faith afloat, to be reminders for the renewal of our courage. The trouble is that our beliefs don't always fulfill that function. Sometimes, instead of buoying up our faith, beliefs weigh it down. What causes that? The answer is: fear.

Faith is trust and courage. Its opposite is fear— or, rather, fearfulness, unhealthy fear. What, do you think, is the most often repeated commandment in the Bible? Think twice. It is this: "Fear not!—Be not afraid!" If it is the courage of faith that makes us perfect, what we must most urgently get rid of is fear. Faith courageously sets out toward the Promised Land, but fear holds on to anything it can get hold of, and so it weighs us down, slows us down. Faith is courage to let go. Fear clings.

There is something healthy in this clinging of fear. Doctors or midwives sometimes test a newborn baby by shaking the table on which it is lying or by causing it a little fear in some other way. If it is a healthy baby, it will, in its fear, reach up with arms and legs and make a grabbing gesture, reaching instinctively for the mother. This reflex is an ancient one. It goes back in our phylogenetic history to a time when we were still living in the trees and had to hang on for dear life, as soon as we were born, to our mothers, who were leaping from branch to branch.

Because our instinct to cling when we get frightened is so ancient, it is deeply ingrained in us. As newborn babies we reach out for our mother; later we hang on to her apron strings, and even as adults, when we panic, we find ourselves instinctively holding on to the next best thing we can grab, even to a complete stranger who might be standing next to us. But this is only the bodily expression of a psychological clinging. The moment we get frightened our mind, too, grabs for anything that promises stability, and clings to it.

From this angle, we might get a clearer view of the relationship between faith and beliefs. Faith, at heart, is fearless trust. When we lose heart, faith weakens and fear mounts. But a fearful mind will compulsively cling to some support. Religious beliefs are readily at hand. They seem to be more stable than anything else we could grab. And so, as faith grows weaker, we clutch our beliefs more and more tightly, more and more rigidly. Sometimes you meet people who seem so compulsive in their effort to convince everyone else of their *beliefs* that it makes you wonder about their *faith*. It sounds too much like whistling in the dark. A person of genuine faith can afford to be far more at ease. Genuine faith holds its beliefs firmly, yes, but ever so lightly.

This is how Abraham, our Father in Faith, held his beliefs. We read about this in Chapter 22 of Genesis. What a marvel of storytelling that chapter is, quite apart from its message! God calls Abraham and sends him on an errand. Now, this time, it is not merely a call to go forth in trust that God will, later on, fill in the details. This time the decisive point is spelled out so precisely that it makes me shudder each time I read it. God orders Abraham to go and sacrifice his son as "a whole-burnt-offering." The message is clear. No margin of error is left. There can be no doubt about the identity of the selected victim: "Take your son." (Abraham had two sons at that time. There was room for doubt, then.) ". . . your only one." (When it comes to sacrificing a child, that child is "the only one" in the parents' mind, no matter how many others they might have.) ". . . the one you love." (That cuts to the quick, but there is still a flicker of hope, until the name is out:) ". . . Isaac!" (It must have hit Abraham like a sword blow.)

This time Abraham's faith is given a definite content. This time faith demands both, believing *in God* as well as believing *something,* something almost unbelievable: Isaac must be sacrificed. Abraham believes that. And yet he had already been promised by God that, through that same Isaac, his offspring would be as numerous as the sands on the seashore, as numerous as the stars in the sky. And Abraham believes that, too. Had Abraham's faith been no more than the sum total of his beliefs, he would have been shipwrecked on their apparent contradictions. But his faith was simple trust in God, who is simple. All contradictions sank into the fathomless simplicity of that faith. He was able therefore, to find support in his belief that God would give him abundant offspring through Isaac, while holding lightly, for the moment, to his belief that this same Isaac was doomed to be sacrificed. His simple faith gave him courage enough to hold both beliefs firmly and trust enough to hold them lightly.

And then comes that incomparable passage, that spine-chilling dialogue between Abraham and Isaac on their way up the mountain of sacrifice. The son carries the firewood for the burnt-offering on his shoulders. The father carries the fire and the knife. "And the two went together." Even the story teller seems to have a lump in his throat, as he repeats: "They went together." Who is without memory of a bus terminal, or a hospital room, where all of life seemed to hang on being "together," as the moment of parting came close? "So, the two went together." The old man walks in silence. What could he possibly say? But the boy speaks up: "Father." "What is it, son?" And now he questions Abraham, not about his faith, but about the content of that faith; not about his trust in God, but about his beliefs; about something which God had spelled out all too clearly, yet something which is apt to shake Abraham's trust in God. Abraham's faith is tested by his beliefs. This is a crucial moment in the history of faith.

Like any bright boy might do, Isaac points out to his father: "Look, here is fire and here is wood, but where is the lamb for the sacrifice?" There is no way out for Abraham. Now he has to prove his faith by confessing what he believes. The son was bright enough to shy away from mentioning the knife in Abraham's hand. Will the father be brave enough *not* to shy away from making clear to Isaac what God made clear to him? At this crucial point, our Father in Faith rises to his full stature: "God will provide himself a lamb, son." It is as if Abraham were thinking: "As far as I can see, God has left no doubt who that lamb will be. But I trust that there may be infinitely more to God's message, than I have understood." Abraham's faith is so strong that he need not cling to his beliefs. His trust in God is stronger than his trust in his own understanding of God's word. In faith he raises his eyes above the horizon of his beliefs.

"And Abraham lifted up his eyes." There is the key word. He does hold his beliefs firmly. He acts on them. But he does not allow his beliefs to become a ballast that weighs down his faith. He looks up.

The story describes in gruesome detail how Abraham binds Isaac's feet together, lays him on the altar, and stretches out his hand to seize the knife to kill his son. All this had to be spelled out, point by point, so as to prove: Abraham acted on God's word;

he did believe. But he had more than belief; he had faith. Believing, he reached down for the knife, but in faith he looked up. "And Abraham lifted up his eyes, and saw, and behold! a ram caught by its horns in a bush. And Abraham went and took the ram and sacrificed it as a burnt-offering instead of Isaac, his son."

What does "instead" mean in this context? It has a twofold significance. Outwardly, it means that the lamb was substituted for Isaac, but the inner meaning is that the lamb represented Isaac. In that sense, Abraham did sacrifice his son. Must we not assume that the inner act of sacrifice had already been completed in his heart, when his hand was able to reach for the knife? And so, what Abraham believed did come true, in the end, but on the level of the unbelievable. Only faith can rise to that level, a faith that is not mere believing, but, above all, trust.

Abraham's faith, his trust in God, was able to uphold even beliefs that seemed contradictory on the level of mere intellectual reasoning. He raised the eyes of his heart to a higher level and, in the light of God's faithfulness, his heart "reasoned that God was powerful enough to even raise from the dead," as the New Testament (Heb 11:19) will interpret this event. That is why, still at the foot of the mountain, Abraham was able to say to his servants, "We (both of us!) will return to you." He was able to say this in faith. For, on the third day of the journey (the resurrection day), Abraham had already "lifted up his eyes," we are told, and had seen the place of sacrifice from afar.

Forgive me for dwelling on this story at some length. I did so, partly because I am so fond of it, I admit. But the insight it offers into the relationship between faith and beliefs is decisive. It makes us realize the priority that faith as courage and trust has over faith in the sense of beliefs. If we get that priority wrong, beliefs may even get in the way of our faith. But if we get it right, we have direct access to the heart of the matter: the heart of faith is the faith of the heart.

The faith of the heart, our primordial faith, is something we have all experienced in our peak moments of aliveness. How did we experience it? As simple trust, as confidence: trust in life; confidence that we won't be let down. At those moments, when we live from our heart, we are in touch with the heart of things. Spontaneously we realize: "There is faithfulness at the heart of all things," as Oscar Cullmann put it so well. Spoken or unspoken, this conviction of faith is the root from which our beliefs spring. It is the touchstone also to test beliefs. If they are genuine, they will express that core conviction and so serve as helpful reminders. Beliefs can never replace the experience of live faith, but they can help us keep it alive.

When our primordial courage is high, our faith articulates its beliefs and upholds them like banners playing in the wind. Courageous faith is free. As long as, in that freedom of faith, we hold our beliefs, rather than being held (captive) by them, they will, at times, uphold us in turn. When our heart sinks, our faltering faith may be upheld by keeping our eyes on those banners of belief that inspire us with fresh courage. But where trust in "the faithfulness at the heart of all things" is dead, beliefs must replace faith: a showroom full of banners, mere articles of faith.

"There is faithfulness at the heart of all things." Faith, alive and full of courage, is our spontaneous response to that insight. For one timeless moment we touched rock-bottom reality. That is enough to know, once and for all, that we do not stand on quicksand. What courage this experience inspires, whenever we remember it! And, even buried under our forgetfulness, that memory remains alive, like live embers buried deep under ashes. Could we really go on living unless we had, deep down within us somewhere, faith that life will keep its promises? We know: life is faithful. And unless, in our heart of hearts, we trusted that insight, we would not even dare to question and at times to deny its truth. At a given moment, we caught sight of the truth that life is faithful, and faith in that vision keeps us going, even if it is merely a glimpse.

Starting from this "given" situation, we might draw out the lines toward a faithful Giver, toward God. Or else we might decline to do so. That is a matter of beliefs. But, in either case, we do have faith in a basic faithfulness. Proof: we go on living.

No one could survive without that basic trust which is the faith all human beings have. This faith is one aspect of grateful aliveness; it is the courage of gratefulness.

What does gratefulness have to do with courage? We might, at a first glance fail to see a connection. But looking more closely it becomes clear that no one can say "thank you" for a gift and mean it, without trust in the giver; and to trust always takes courage. Take a simple example. A friend hands you a gift-wrapped package, and you say "thank you." You might think that you have expressed your appreciation for the gift. But wait! You haven't even looked at what's inside that package. How could you express your appreciation? What you really expressed was trust in your friend. A grateful person will say "thank you" before checking what's inside the gift-wrapping. If you wait to express your thanks until after you have examined the gift, you might be smart, but no one will call you grateful. True gratefulness is courage to give thanks for a gift before unwrapping it.

Now, it might not cost you a great amount of courage to trust your friend. True enough, that box wrapped in gold paper is just the right size to contain a medium-large time bomb. But who would even dream of that possibility? When life hands you a gift, however, it's a more serious matter. God has a way of putting time bombs into pretty packages. We know that from past experience, and now we get another one of those surprise gifts. To be there to say "thank you" and mean it does take courage. It is as if you were saying: "Watch it! This might be another one of those whoppers. It might blow me to pieces. But even if it does, I trust that this is just what I need right now." That's trust all right! And that trust in the Giver is the crucial point where faith and gratefulness meet.

Once we have discovered that the courage of gratefulness and the courage of faith are one and the same movement of the heart, a gesture of trust, we can also see that learning faith will mean learning gratefulness. Now we are in a better position to answer the question with which we started this chapter: How can we learn to live gratefully? By learning to grow in faith. The advantage of this approach should be easy to see. To speak of grateful living sounds far less abstract than to speak of a life of faith. It appeals to experience rather than to theological categories. Grateful living is, however, a poorly defined territory. What tradition says about faith provides us with the kind of map we mentioned earlier. Growth in faith is something that is well mapped out. Our journey is difficult enough. We better use the help tradition has to offer through its insights concerning faith.

By now we have drawn the line between faith and beliefs clearly enough to realize that growth in faith does not mean accumulation of beliefs. It means, rather, learning to make the basic gesture of faith in more and more difficult circumstances, in circumstances in which the faithfulness to which faith responds is less and less obvious. In the end we ought to be able to trust in that "faithfulness at the heart of all things" even when we cannot see it at all. In this sense, and in this sense alone, does it make sense to speak of blind faith. But that means that blind faith has the most penetrating vision. Blind faith sees nothing and can, nevertheless, truthfully say, "I see!" See what? Nothing. No thing, but the meaning of all things, namely: faithfulness at the core of all.

Looking up to those heights of faith might tend to discourage us before we ever start. But our ascent begins in the valley. I am reminded of hikes in the Austrian Alps, where I grew up. We would set out early on a summer morning. And there, before us, snow covered, in the first light of dawn rose those icy peaks and ridges that were our goal. But all around us lay lush pasture land, and buttercups were nodding in the breeze that always springs up just before sunrise. Our journey of faith starts on easy ground. And that is just as well. The task is difficult enough. Why shouldn't we begin with the easiest steps?

The ascent of faith is a prayerful ascent. That means: Every time we move another step, every time we repeat the inner gesture of courage and trust, we do not only exercise faith, we tap the very source of faithfulness that gives us strength to go on. Drinking from that source is prayer: the Prayer of Faith. Another name for it is "Living by the Word of God."

When the Bible speaks of "living by the Word of God," there is more to it than the idea that God gives the word of command and we live according to it. This is merely the moral aspect of this great biblical concept. The religious aspect (always in danger of being swallowed up by the moral one) is infinitely more important. Living by the Word of God means feeding on it, being nourished by it, eating, drinking, and assimilating that Word. The image of food and drink is always closely associated with living by the Word. We have similar expressions in English. When someone pays close attention to every word of a story, we say, "She ate it all up," or "He lapped it all up." There is the eating and the drinking. Or we might say of a book, "I devoured it, cover to cover." That image of eating up a book is also biblical. In fact, it occurs both in the Old and the New Testament (Ez 3:1; Rev 10:10).

The idea behind all this is one of the deepest insights in the Bible: God speaks. What does this mean? It is image language, of course. But what experience stands behind the idea that God speaks? It is the experience of listening with our heart. For there is an aspect to that experience which we overlook all too easily. When we truly listen with the heart, we do not merely overhear something that is going on "out there," with or without us, regardless. No. We find ourselves addressed. We realize in a flash: Whatever is "out there" concerns us, because it is somehow concerned with us, it is "toward" us in some mysterious way. This is just another way of

speaking, gropingly, about faithfulness at the heart
of all things. If we want, then, to put this insight into
God-language, its most concise formulation is: God
speaks.

But God is too simple to say more than one
Word. All that God says is expressed, as it were, in
the one eternal Word of faithfulness. That one
Word, however, is so inexhaustibly pregnant with
meaning that it needs to be spelled out forever and
ever in all that is. It is as with faithful lovers. All they
want so say to one another is: "I love you." But that
bears repetition. No lover is ever going to say:
"Well, I love you. Didn't I tell you so, once and for
all, years ago? Do you really want to hear it again?"
Yes, we do want to hear it over and over again. And
lovers will go on expressing their faithfulness not
only in words, but in gifts, in flowers, in songs, in
letters, in caresses, in a thousand different ways, a
lifetime long. In a similar way God's faithfulness
needs to be spelled out in ever new forms forever
and ever. Everything there is in the whole universe
exists for no other reason than to get this message
across. In faith the heart intuits this secret.

God's message is always the same. But the way
the message is expressed makes all the difference.
You may perceive the message in an apple orchard
in full bloom. But the same message is also there in a
forest fire. The difference would be bewildering,
but to discover the same message in different dis-
guises turns it all into a delightful game, a spelling
game. That horse frolicking in the meadow is one

way to spelling out God's Word; the cat asleep in my lap is another. Each is unique, untranslatable. Poems can't be translated; they can at best be approximated in a different language. In a poem the language counts as much as the message. God is the poet. If we want to know what God says in a tomato, we must look at a tomato, feel it, smell it, bite into it, have the juice and seeds squirt all over us when it pops. We must savor it and learn this tomato poem "by heart." But what God must say can't be exhausted in tomato language. So, God gives us lemons and speaks in Lemonese. Living by the Word means learning God's languages, one by one, a lifetime long.

This is the easy, first stage of the prayer of faith, its joyful mysteries. We are still on the stretch of our ascent that leads through the meadows, barely sloping upward. And yet even this stage of living by the Word demands courage. Look at little Johnny's face when for the first time he bites into a tomato. How that telltale face reports, blow by blow, the struggle between the fearful reluctance and the venturesome courage of exploring unknown territory. Starting with our first breath, every new encounter with the world implies trust in the faithfulness at the heart of all things. No matter how hidden, or implicit, this trust may be, it is proof of our primoridal faith. It is the beginning of faith in fullness. And no matter how weak that faith may be, it will grow, step by step. That bite into your first tomato did take courage, but that courage was rewarded. Without daring there is not adventure. But adventure becomes the reward of our daring. The ancient faithfulness at the heart of things is always a brand-new surprise. And as we savor it anew, faithfulness strengthens our faith and makes it grow. That grateful feasting of faith at the banquet of faithfulness is the prayer of faith, living by the Word, a holy communion.

The banquet of life is the challenge to cultivate and broaden our taste. Every one of us begins with a provincial taste. Life challenges us to acquire a cosmopolitan, a truly catholic taste. In this learning process, some of us falter at the simplest exercises. Think, for instance, of the weather. With every change of weather a new adventure awaits us; each new season has its own recipes for dishing up new surprises. And we? It is our privilege, of course, to have our preferences, our favorite dishes. But is one man's meat really another one's poison? "Try it; you'll like it," comes closer to the truth. It could pass for a contemporary version of "Taste and perceive how good the Lord is." In order to taste and perceive, I must dare to taste first. Perceiving the goodness is the reward for the courage to taste. But to give ourselves to the sea breeze on a spring day is one thing; to step out into the mist and fog of a winter morning with the same sense of adventure demands more courage. Yet, if we draw back, how can we ever taste the unique flavor that only fog can convey to our heart, as it hides and reveals, conceals and shows again trees with dripping twigs and people in raincoats with dripping noses. How much of life is lost on us unless we can enjoy every kind of weather in its own way?

How can we expect to find life in fullness unless we learn to live "by *every* word that comes from the mouth of God"? That is a crucial passage in the Gospels—crucial for all who seek fullness of life, crucial for anyone who wants to learn grateful living. Which do I want to do? Pick and choose which word of God to live by? After all, who knows best what's good for me, if not I myself? Or do I trust that God knows better and that God will speak precisely that word which I need, even though I might not like to hear it just now? The faith of gratefulness trusts in the Giver and, therefore, has the courage to say, "I can live by every word that comes from the mouth of God."

This passage comes from the Gospel story called the temptation of Jesus. He has spent forty days and forty nights in the desert, re-enacting the forty years of Israel's desert wanderings. He has been fasting, a gesture of total reliance on God. Israel relied on God, and God provided manna, bread from heaven in the desert. But Jesus is hungry and God provides nothing but stones for Him. What father will give his hungry children stones when they cry for bread? If God cared with a father's tenderness for Israel, why not for this Israelite who calls on God with such deep confidence as "Abba," Father? If He is truly God's Son, is not all that He needs His for the asking? A tempting thought. But Jesus turns it around: This is how I show my faith as Son in the Father: not by asking to get what I need, but by trusting that I need what I get. God knows best. When God says "stones," I will not insist that the word should be "bread." I can live by *every* word. . . .

But can I really? This is where things get tough. Now we are out of the meadows, and our ascent gets steep. These are no longer beginners' exercises in faith. Here we are confronted with a life-and-death issue. The biblical symbolism makes this clear. Bread stands for life, stones for death. Jesus trusts that every word of God is life-giving. The word in question here is stones. It spells death. The implication is: I can live even by dying.

This theme is picked up in a different Gospel story, the agony of Jesus in the garden, another temptation story, if you want. In both stories living by the Word is the crucial issue. In both cases the word, which God speaks, spells death. Stones are all the Father offers in the desert, not bread; in the garden he offers the chalice, another symbol for the death sentence, as it is in the Psalms. This time it is a hard struggle for Jesus: "Father, if it is possible, let this chalice pass me by—yet, not my will be done, but yours." This is the prayer of faith in its sorrowful mysteries. With bloody sweat Jesus struggles through to a faith that trusts in finding God's faithfulness even at the core of death.

Sooner or later, each of us must reach this level

of faith. Maybe God is still preparing us for that
steep part of the climb. At the beginning, Living by
the Word is pure delight: God feeds us not only with
bread, but raisin bread, as it were. And for a long
time our trust is built up in this way. But sooner or
later comes the moment when we bite into that
raisin bread, and what we took to be a raisin turns
out to be a small pebble. That is the crucial moment,
the moment of testing for our faith. What am I going
to say? Am I going to protest that I can't live by
stones? Or has my faith grown strong enough by
now that, after meditating on the joyful mysteries
for so long, I can pass over to the sorrowful ones?
When, for the first time, God says "stones," where I
expected to hear "bread" do I have the faith to say:
"I can live by *every* word that comes from the
mouth of God"?

Most of us have been tested in this way. An
unexpected turn of fate, a seemingly impossible task
looming up before us, the loss of a friend—a word
that spells death. "This is going to kill me," we say.
And we are right. It is going to kill at least some part
of us. Yet, our response to this word is what counts.
Experience tells us that in situations of this kind we
can shrivel up in fear and our life will be dimin-
ished. But experience also teaches us that we can
step out in faith and "get our teeth into it," yes,
even into rocks. We might still be killed in the
process, but we come out of this experience more
alive. Living by the Word means courage to "eat it

all up." If we can do this, while being killed, "death is swallowed up," as St. Paul says. "Death is swallowed up in victory"—by faith.

There is no telling how many times in the course of a lifetime we may have to go through this process of creative dying. (The more creatively we live, the more often we shall have to die, I suppose.) But one thing is certain: in the end, no one can be spared this passage. There is a staggering variety of dishes set out on the banquet table of life. Each one of us gets a different menu. The final course, however, is the same for all of us: It is one big rock. "Sorry," says our Host, "but now it's time to die." Will we be ready by then to "swallow up death"? If so, it will be a dying into fullness of life. We know this. We know it, not because someone else told us so, but because we have experienced it in one way or another. From our partial experiences of dying, we learn to expect a similar pattern in our final death. We learn that faith is the power to die into greater aliveness every time we get killed. And so we have reason to expect that being fully killed will mean coming fully alive. How? We cannot tell. If we knew, there would be no room for faith. But we know all we need to know: Faith finds life in every word of God, even when that word spells death.

Every creative death experience, no matter how small, teaches us how to rise to the third level of our ascent in faith, the glorious mysteries of Living by the Word. Now we are among those snowy peaks that looked so frightening from below. And, in a way, they are even more frightening now. But our courage has grown strong enough to enjoy it all. There is no more birdsong. There are no more flowers. Only the sky (blue almost black in contrast to the glacier peaks), silence, and fierce sun. But it is pure ecstasy.

Let me try to use a different illustration for what I call the ascent of faith. A youthful friendship starts out with joyful mysteries. The more fully we explore them, the broader will be the basis for what might grow into a lifelong love. Day by day we drink with new delight from one another's lips, bathe in the light of one another's eyes. But sooner or later friendship leads into sorrowful mysteries. There is no growing without dying to what we have outgrown. And even the closest friends cannot always grow at the same pace. If we have the courage to let go of each other, this death experience will become creative. If I remain faithful (not necessarily the other, but I), we shall find each other again on a level we could never have imagined. And every time we pass through this kind of death, we catch a glimpse of the glorious mysteries that lie beyond. If in the first days of our friendship a time machine would have shown us the other's face a half century later, we would hardly have had the courage to go on. But now we look into that old face and see a beauty more thrilling than on the day we first met.

In the end, life strips the last shreds of husk

from the kernel of faithfulness at the heart of all things. But at first, and for a long time, we need that husk. While it is still green, it is the husk that attracts us. Yet, all the time faith feeds on the kernel and slowly grows strong enough to do without the husk. Slowly we learn to make sense of life and that sense goes far beyond what our senses can reach. And I'm not talking about abstract concepts. Life simply begins to make sense to the heart, heart-sense. And that comes through faith. But how can our faith ever grow strong unless we start with the joyful mysteries, Living by the Word in ways that are pure delight? Any other start is apt to lead to impoverishment.

Even people who think of themselves as serious seekers often end up with sadly impoverished lives. Though one can't be too serious in one's search, one can be serious in the wrong way. There is nothing more serious than play. Children know that. And the child within us never forgets it. You can tell true seriousness from glumness by its playfulness. To seek seriously means to seek playfully. And the joyful mysteries of Living by the Word teach us this playfulness. By far the largest part of the exercises in faith consists of learning God's games. If we insist that God ought to be more serious than that, we'll miss the fun of it all. In fact, we'll miss the point of everything. (The point of everything? Well, that's the point at the heart of each thing where the kernel of faithfulness is playfully hidden.)

Martin Buber tells a story that is precisely to the point in question:

> Rabbi Barukh's grandson Yehiel was once play-
> ing hide-and-seek with another boy. He hid
> himself well and waited for his playmate to find
> him. When he had waited for a long time, he
> came out of his hiding place, but the other was
> nowhere to be seen. Now Yehiel realized that
> he had not looked for him from the very begin-
> ning. This made him cry, and crying he ran to
> his grandfather and complained of his faithless
> friend. Then tears brimmed in Rabbi Barukh's
> eyes and he said: "God says the same thing: 'I
> hide, but no one wants to seek me.'"

If our seriousness is a playful seriousness, much of our life of faith will be child's play, delight upon delight. Once the child within us has learned the game, we'll be able to see the point also when the sorrowful mysteries begin. With a child's simplicity, we'll go right to the heart of the matter and find that here, too, it is all a game of hide-and-seek. Death (and each one of the many deaths in the course of life) is the point where I so completely lose myself in the seeking that a breakthrough occurs: I find. But what I find is not what I was looking for. I find that what I was after, without knowing it, wasn't finding at all, but being found. And at that moment I am found. Yes, now I even found myself, but that seems no longer of much importance in the midst of these glorious mysteries.

Seeking, losing myself, and allowing myself to be found—it is all child's play. Why then don't I do it? The answer is: I am afraid—afraid of seeking, and maybe not finding; afraid of losing myself, maybe for good; afraid of being found and maybe found wanting. Maybe I'm afraid, most of all, that there must be something wrong with so childlike an approach. I'm afraid it can't be that simple. In short, I'm afraid period. Thus, once again, how can I overcome my fearfulness?

Just two suggestions in answer to that crucial question. The first was implicit in what we just discussed. We learn faith step by little step, and at the same pace we overcome fearfulness. By tackling the fear for which we are just strong enough, we grow stronger and can tackle the next one. As a small boy I used to be afraid of the dark. My mother knew it and would send me to pick up her sewing basket from the garden bench after nightfall. I ran and whistled to give myself courage. But in doing so I found out that nothing frightful happened. And I gained courage to tackle another fear.

Maybe we should, now and then, make a list of our fears—all of them. Of course there will be many reasonable fears among them, legitimate fears; we'll leave those alone. And when in doubt, let's give ourselves the benefit of the doubt. Let's assume that our fears are reasonable and legitimate, unless the contrary is pretty obvious. There will still be enough unreasonable fears left on our list. We may be sure of that. And those are the ones we want to look at more closely. Maybe there is one among them we'll dare to tackle after all, even if it's only our unreasonable fear of spiders or hitchhikers. We pick that one out from our list. For once we do what we fear, and we see that the fear was unfounded. Not only do we survive what we unreasonably feared, but the experience lifts us onto a new and unsuspected level of aliveness. As often as we try this out, we find it to be true.

But I have another suggestion. This one has to do with how we think about our fears. It would be too bad if all this talk about faith and fear merely resulted in adding a new fear to our old ones: the fear of having fears. That would surely be the most unreasonable one of them all. Let's think positively even about our fears. We know that courage presupposes fear. This is true even with the courage of faith. Without fear there is no courage. Children sometimes do things that would demand great courage from an adult. But in the children's case, this exposure to danger is mere stupidity. The more clearly we see the danger, the greater the fear, but the greater also the courage that overcomes our fear.

There is a play, *The Song on the Scaffold,* based on a novel by Gertrud von LeFort, that tells of a community of Carmelite nuns during the French Revolution. Disobeying orders to abandon their religious life, the nuns are imprisoned and led to their execution. So great is their faith and courage that they go up to the scaffold singing. Their song gets softer and softer as one by one the women are beheaded. Only with the last one the song ends. But this is where the core of the story begins. For, as it turns out, the last one to die with her companions was not really the last. One of the nuns had not had the courage to face death. She had gone into hiding. And now she must struggle all alone through agony after agony until she, too, gives herself up to be executed. To the last moment she is full of fear. But in the end it clearly emerges that her courage was greater than that of those who died triumphantly. Because the fear she had to overcome was so much greater, the courage that overcame her fear was greater, too.

We might even think of fear as the headwind of faith. The faster we go, say, on a bicycle, the stronger is the headwind we feel. It is our speed that creates that courage. As long as our faith remains a nose's length ahead of our fear, fine. Let's measure our courage by the fears we manage to master and pat ourselves on the back. We need not fear fear.

The struggle between fear and faith crystallizes into the image of Jesus in His agony. In the Garden of Olives, He becomes "the pioneer of our faith." But this trail-blazing costs Him bloody sweat. In the end He accepts the cup just as He had accepted the stones in place of bread. Are we not invited to see a connection between this bread and cup and the bread and cup of the Lord's Supper? Whenever Christians celebrate the Eucharist, breaking bread and sharing the cup, they celebrate fullness of life. Yes, but with reference to death, with reference to a bloody agony in which faith conquered fear. The Eucharist is a challenge to follow Christ from fear to faith.

The very symbols of the Eucharistic meal are ambiguous symbols. Bread is a symbol of life. The breaking of bread signifies sharing of life that grows in the sharing. And yet the breaking also signifies destruction; it is a reminder of the body broken in death. The cup of blood drained from the body signifies death. But it is also the cup passed around in a festive gathering of friends, in an hour celebrating life. It takes courage to accept this double meaning. Only together can the two aspects stand for fullness.

The courage it takes to receive life even under the image of death—that is the courage of faith, the courage of gratefulness: trust in the Giver. When one approaches the altar to receive the Eucharistic bread and cup, this is an act of courage. It is a gesture by which one says, "I trust that I can live by *every* word that comes from the mouth of God, yes, even the word that spells death." All that remains is to translate that act of faith into daily living. And this is done through gratefulness. Eucharist, after all, means "thanksgiving." As we learn to give thanks for all of life and death, for all of this given world of ours, we find a deep joy. It is the joy of courageous trust, the joy of faith in the faithfulness at the heart of all things. It is the joy of gratefulness in touch with the fullness of life.

Hope: Openness for Surprise

In moments when we are truly alive, we experience life as gift. We also experience life as surprise. Faith is the heart's response to life as gift. The heart's response to life as surprise is hope, as we shall see. The more the insight that life is freely given takes hold of us, the more our life will be a life of faith, a life of trust in the Giver. Of course, that trust itself is gift: God gives us faith to respond to God's own faithfulness. And so we come to understand faith as an aspect of God's own life within us. Hope is another aspect of that same fullness of life. The more the insight that life is surprising takes hold of us, the more our life will be a life of hope, a life of openness for Surprise. And Surprise is a name of God. In fact, Surprise is a somewhat more successful name than others, though all names miss the mark when we aim at naming the Nameless One. Like all other names, the name Surprise fails to name God. But in doing so it succeeds at least in holding our heart open for the insight that such failure can be success.

And this puts us right at the center of the paradox of hope.

Hope, too, is an aspect of God's very life within us. If faith is trust in the Giver (a name of God we quickly recognize), hope is openness for Surprise. The surprise of surprises is God within us.

This makes us ask: How can we grow more open in hope? The poet Rilke looks at the wide open star of an anemone and is struck by the same question. He marvels at the flower-muscle that opens the petals bit by bit to the morning light. That muscle of limitless welcome tensed in the still star of the blossom is sometimes so overwhelmed by the fullness of light that it is scarcely able to pull back the wide-sprung petal-edges when sunset beckons to rest. And we, the poet asks—when, when will *we* at last be open to receive like that?

Again, those moments come to mind when life in fullness overwhelms us. We are surprised by joy. No matter how fleeting the experience is we know now the joy of being open for surprise. For a moment we feel unconditionally welcome, and that makes us able to welcome life unconditionally. The taste of that experience awakens in us a passion for life with its sheer limitless possibilities. That passion is hope: "a passion for the possible."

The phrase, "passion for the possible," was coined by a prophet of hope for our time. It is the last word on the last page of William Sloane Coffin's autobiography, *Once to Every Man*. That book moved me deeply. My love and admiration for the author surely played a part. But, more objectively, I was struck by the way he addressed himself to the crucial issues we must face today. Courageously he takes those issues to heart, with all the pain this brings, and allows that passion (in the double sense of fervor and anguish) to purify his hope.

Life itself will purify our hope step by step if we live with a passion for the possible. As we go forward, the apparent limits of the possible will be pushed back further and further into the region of the seemingly impossible. Sooner or later we realize that the possible has no fixed limits. What we mistook for a limit proves to be a horizon. And, like every horizon, it recedes as we move on toward fullness of life.

This exploration animated by a passion for the possible is, of course, our religious quest, spurred on by the restlessness of our human heart. Hope makes our religious quest what it is. The very notion of quest implies hope. We may start with the definition of hope as "expectant desire." There are events we expect, but do not desire. There are things we desire, but never expect. Expectation by itself is not hope, nor is desire by itself hope. To desire what we do not expect may be a daydream. To expect what we do not desire may be a nightmare. But hope welds our expectancy and desire together and sends us forth, wide awake, on our quest.

There is a healthy restlessness in the quest which hope inspires. Both expectation and desire contain an element of not yet. We see not yet what we expect. We hold not yet what we desire. We are still on the way toward it. And yet both expectation and desire already anticipate the goal. Already we look from afar for what we still expect. We set our heart on what we still desire. (The word "desire," derived from the Latin *sidus*, "star," suggests hitching your heart to a star.) The not-yet keeps our quest restless. The already keeps that restlessness healthy.

How difficult it is to live in the creative tension of hope, the tension between not-yet and already! When we allow that tension to snap, our quest peters out in aimless wandering or gets stuck in a compulsive settling down. We see this all around us, even among religious folk. There are those who want everything already. They cannot be bothered with a not-yet. Getting there is all that matters to them. They want things settled once and for all, and the sooner the better. Searching is a nuisance for them. Their counterparts, on the other hand, are so enamored with searching that finding becomes a threat. Finding would put an end to the search. It would spoil the game. The thrill they find in the quest lies exclusively in the not-yet.

The compulsive settler stresses one pole of the great quest at the expense of the opposite pole, which the aimless wanderer stresses. Hope is thereby polarized.

Compulsive settlers are too fearful of the hazards of traveling. Can we blame them? They have a greater awareness of the dangers by which the search is beset. Aimless wanderers in turn are more aware how much it costs us to commit ourselves to a goal. Can we blame them for being too fearful of that commitment? We should rather admire the settlers for their courage to commit themselves and admire the wanderers for their courage to be on the way. But then we must go one step further and imitate what we admire in both. This double courage must overcome fear by faith so that hope can come into its own. And this is merely another way of saying that faith precedes hope.

Great and justified is the fear of dangers that could befall us on the road; even more so is the fear of risking commitment. We can never fully assess the courage it costs to overcome that double fear by faith. We overcome by joining the daring of the wanderer to the daring of the settler, and that gives us the courage of a pilgrim. The compulsive settler within us dares to be committed, but fears being on the road. The aimless wanderer within us dares to be on the road, but fears being committed. Only the pilgrim within us overcomes that polarization. The pilgrim knows that each step on the road may prove to be the goal, yet the goal may prove to have been but one step on the road. This keeps the pilgrim open for surprise. Hope is openness for surprise. Hope is the virtue of the pilgrim.

Leo Tolstoy tells the story of two old men, Russian peasants, who go on a pilgrimage to Jerusalem. For many weeks they walk together from village to village, making their way toward the Black Sea, where they expect to take a ship for the Holy Land.

But before they reach the seaport, they get separated. While one of them stops at a cottage to get a drink of water, the other one walks ahead for a while, then sits down in the shade, and soon falls asleep. When he wakes up he wonders: "Is my friend still behind me? No, he must have passed by while I was sleeping here." Hoping to catch up with his fellow pilgrim, he walks on. "At least while waiting for a ship we shall meet again," he thinks. But in the harbor there is no trace of his friend. He waits for days, but then sails for the Holy Land alone.

Only in Jerusalem does our pilgrim catch up with the other one. He sees him up near the altar, but before he can push his way through the crowd of pilgrims, he loses his friend again. He asks for him, but no one knows where he is staying. Once more he sees him in the crowd, and a third time, closer to the holy places than he can get. He never catches up with him though, and when it is time to leave Jerusalem, he must set out on his journey home alone.

Many months later he returns to the village where their pilgrimage began. And there is his lost travel companion. He had not been to Jerusalem— not in his body at least. What he found in that cottage where he stopped for water was a whole family at the point of death. They were poor and in debt, sick, famished, and too weak even to fetch water for themselves. Compassion overwhelmed him. He went to bring them water, bought food, and nursed them back to health. Each day he thought, "Tomorrow I will continue my pilgrimage." But after he helped them pay their debts, he was left with just enough money to return home. On hearing this side of the story, the old man who saw his fellow pilgrim in Jerusalem could not help wondering which of them had reached the true goal of their pilgrimage.

In the Bible we find, again and again, one key image for the quest of the heart: the image of the way. This image will yield a deeper significance if we keep in mind that the biblical way is always the way of a pilgrim. It is the way on which one step, surprisingly, may lead us to the goal, and the goal may turn out to be, surprisingly, the first of many further steps on the road. The image of the way tells us that we need not fear losing the thrill of the search, even though we find. Nor need we fear losing the joyous possession of what we have found, even though there is no end to exploring. T.S. Eliot, in his *Four Quartets*, speaks of the paradox of being "still and still moving," the paradox of hope. So keen are his insights and so powerfully expressed, that I would like to insert some of Eliot's poetic lines into my own groping attempts to speak about hope.

> We shall not cease from exploration
> And the end of all our exploring
> Will be to arrive where we started
> And know the place for the first time.

"We shall not cease from exploration," because to be "on the way" means being on the move. It makes little difference whether we sit down on the wrong way or on the right one. As long as we are sitting, we are not on the way to anywhere. Whenever we get comfortably settled, God says: "Your ways are not my ways" (Is 55:8). That shatters our illusory security and puts us back out into the cold, on the dark road. And that is a blessing. The real threat is that God may let us have it our way until we are nauseated by what we most desired. To be stuck in what we have found is no better than losing ourselves in the seeking. Sooner or later we begin to realize that our finding is not really what matters, but our being found. We come to see that our knowing the way is not what matters, but our being known. In biblical terms, the righteous may come to know the way only gropingly, but "the Lord knows the way of the righteous" (Ps 1:6), and that is what counts.

As pilgrims we have a goal. But the meaning of our pilgrimage does not depend on reaching that goal. It depends on remaining open in hope, open for surprise, because God knows our way far better than we do. In that knowledge our heart finds rest while we keep moving on. Hope as the virtue of the pilgrim accounts for both stillness and movement. True, our expectant desire sets us in motion. "Desire itself is movement/not in itself desirable" (*Four Quartets*). But the stillness in which we "rest in hope" (Ps 16:9) is certainly not something reserved for those who have reached the goal by reaching the end of the road. On a pilgrimage, the goal is present in every step along the road, because the end precedes the beginning. Resting in hope, we move, according to T.S. Eliot, in a dynamic stillness:

> ... as a Chinese jar still
> Moves perpetually in its stillness.
> Not the stillness of the violin, while the note lasts,
> Not that only, but the co-existence,
> Or say that the end precedes the beginning,
> And the end and the beginning were always there
> Before the beginning and after the end.
> And all is always now. ...

The tension of hope, poised between the already and the not-yet, is basic for an understanding of the pilgrim's way. It is basic for that quest for meaning that is the pilgrimage of every human heart. Whenever we find something meaningful, its meaning is given already and not yet. It is there, but there is always more to it. One doesn't find meaning as one finds blueberries in some clearing in the woods—as something to pick, take home, and turn into preserves. Meaning is always fresh. We find it suddenly like the discovery of a unique shaft of afternoon light slanting out of low clouds and onto this same clearing in the woods. In its light we can discover ever new marvels as long as we keep looking.

St. Paul speaks of the infinitely unfolding splendor of meaning as "hope of glory" (2 Cor 1:29). We shall examine the connection between hope and glory later on. In our present context it seems important to note that St. Paul thinks of this hope of glory as already and not-yet. On the one hand, it is "Christ in you" (*ibid.*), the Christ life at the very core of our aliveness. Thus, it is something already intimately given. Yet, at the same time, that life of ours is still "hidden with Christ in God" (Col 3:3), the God of boundless possibilities, of future, of surprise, of hope. "*Already* we are children of God; what we shall be has *not yet* come to light" (1 Jn 3:2). We are still on the way. But that way is Christ.

The Ground of Being, the Matrix of all there is, the invisible God is "God of hope" (Rom 15:13). Therefore, the "image of the invisible God" (Col 1:15) must be "Way" (Jn 14:6), the perfect symbol of hope. Those who move on that "new and living way" (Heb 10:20) "abound in hope, through the power of the Holy Spirit (Rom 15:13). As we reflect on those passages, we realize how hope is rooted in the very mystery of the Triune God. The Father from whom we come and to whom we go is "God of hope." The Son in whom we live and who lives in us is "our hope." The Holy Spirit, God's very life within us, gives us the power to hope.

The Spirit of God fills the whole universe and draws all of creation into that great movement of unfolding hope. St. Paul describes this cosmic upsurge of hope in his Letter to the Romans, Chapter 8, verses 14–25, a passage worth rereading in this context. God is and is coming. The already and the not-yet coincide in God. We may think of the God of hope as "still and still moving." Hope, as God's life within us, unfolds in that creative tension. T.S. Eliot says:

> We must be still and still moving
> Into another intensity
> For a further union, a deeper communion. . . .

The surprise within the surprise of every new discovery is that there is ever more to be discovered. Hope holds the present open for an ever fresh future. Let us remember, however, that it makes no sense to speak of past and future with regard to God. God lives in "the now that does not pass away." Reflected into time, God's now unfolds for us as past, present, and future. As an aspect of God's life, hope "lasts" (1 Cor 13:13). As experienced within us, hope is in a special way related to the future. Hope holds us open in a twofold sense: for a future in time and for a future beyond time, God's now. That divine future does not come later. Hope opens us to it by making every moment "the point of intersection of the timeless/with time" (*Four Quartets*). Eliot also speaks of:

> . . . the sudden illumination—
> We had the experience but missed the meaning,
> And approach to the meaning restores the
>   experience
> In a different form. . . .

Hope has power to transform even the past by discovering in it new meaning.

What might have been and what has been
Point to one end, which is always present.

That end is the meaning of all. And the mode in
which it is present is hope.

Theological reflections like the ones in which
we have been engaged just now have their place. St.
Peter exhorts us: "Be ready at all times to answer
anyone who asks you to give an account of the hope
you have within you" (1 Pet 3:15). But loving is
ultimately the only account one can give of love.
What faith is like can best be shown by being faithful. And so with hope. Nothing will help us understand hope as much as a pilgrim's life, "still and still
moving," day by day. And nothing will be as convincing to others as the way we exercise hope in our
inner attitude and in our outward behavior. Let us
therefore look at the mooring hope provides for our
life.

Hope is realistic. The realism of hope is humility. Most of us think of realism as a virtue. But
humility? It is time to reclaim that beautiful term
from pietistic jargon. After all, humility is directly
related to "humus" and to an earthiness we are
rediscovering today. Humility is down-to-earth. It is,
therefore, related also to "humor" and to plain "hu-
manness." Only when we are down-to-earth can we
laugh about ourselves; and that makes us human.

The etymological connections may be doubtful. But the psychological connections hold. The truly human is marked by the humor of humble realism. And that humor is the most winning aspect of hope.

Wouldn't it seem, though, at first sight that pessimism is more realistic than hope? It would seem so to the pessimist at least. But the optimists assure us that pessimists are unrealistic. And the pessimists, in turn, claim that they themselves are optimists—with more realistic information. Statistical evidence seems to suggest that there is probably one pessimist for every optimist. Why don't we allow them to cancel each other out and, realistically, start from scratch?

On closer inspection, optimism and pessimism are equally unrealistic. Neither optimists nor pessimists are much concerned with reality, only with holding their party line. Their concern is to strike their characteristic pose regardless of the facts they face. Optimism and pessimism pretend. But hope shows concern. If optimist and pessimist are politicians, hope is a mother. A mother does not pose. She does not pretend. Hope does not even pretend that everything will be all right. Hope simply does its thing, like that spider in the corner of my bookshelf. She will make a new web again and again, as often as my feather duster swooshes it away—without self-pity, without self-congratulations, without expectations, without fear. If I could achieve the corresponding attitude on my level of consciousness, that would be hope all right. It would cost me more. On my level the stakes are higher. But I bow to that spider.

Many of us tend to think that optimism is at least a little closer to hope than pessimism is. That is not so. Luckily, we do not have to choose between optimism and pessimism. But if we must make a choice, pessimism would be preferable, and this on two counts. For one, it is easy to mistake optimism for genuine hope. With pessimism we are safe from that deception. And then, if we are pleasantly stupid, we can get hopelessly stuck in optimism. Pessimism tends to become so unbearable, even for the pessimist, that it can catapult one right into hope, when it snaps.

Some people imagine that hope is the highest degree of optimism, a kind of super-optimism. I get the image of someone climbing higher and higher to the most fanciful pinnacle of optimism, there to wave the little flag of hope. A far more accurate picture would be that hope happens when the bottom drops out of our pessimism. We have nowhere to fall but into the ultimate reality of God's motherly caring. That is why St. Paul tells us that "tribulation leads to patience; and patience to experience; and experience to hope" (Rom 5:3f). Will this chain reaction be likely to work unless we have at least a little hope to start with? I, for one, do need a little hope in tribulation to keep me from losing my patience altogether. Yes, but this initial hope may still have a generous dose of optimism mixed into it. The ordeal of experience must purge out all dross of posing and pretense in a slow burning fire. Only then will hope show its mettle and ring true.

This process of purgation is at the core of every spiritual discipline. Patience holds still in the blast-furnace of experience. Discipline is not so much a matter of doing this or that, but of holding still. Not as if this would cost no effort. But the effort is all applied to the crucial task, the task of making no effort. In the words of Eliot in *Four Quartets*:

> I said to my soul, be still and wait without hope
> For hope would be hope for the wrong thing; wait
>   without love
> For love would be love of the wrong thing; there is
>   yet faith
> But the faith and the love and the hope are all in
>   the waiting.

The disciple waiting on the master is silent. The pupil, eye-to-eye with the teacher, is all attention. This stillness is not a shutting up. It is the stillness of the anemone wide open to the sunlight. Even the clatter of thoughts is silenced by the discipline of this stillness. Says Eliot:

> Wait without thought, for you are not ready for
>   thought;
> So the darkness shall be the light, and the stillness
>   the dancing.

The Dance Master of spiritual discipline is a most demanding teacher. The stillness and the darkness in which hope is purified is a "condition of complete simplicity/(costing not less than everything)" *(Four Quartets)*. The image of dance suggests an aspect of hope which Joseph Pieper, the masterful writer on this virtue, has pointed out: Hope is closely related to youthfulness. This is true not only in the sense that we expect young people to be full of hope. Old people, if they have learned the virtue of hope, radiate an unexpected youthfulness. "Therefore, we do not grow faint," St. Paul writes; "even though outwardly we wear out, inwardly we grow younger day by day" (2 Cor 4:16). Dancing rejuvenates us.

In the youthfulness of hope the stillness of waiting is one with the dancing. Little tots are too clumsy to dance and too impatient to wait. ("My sister's almost ten, I mean nine, because she's eight," said my little friend Peter, who can't wait for his own next birthday.) Old folk tend to wonder what's left worth waiting for, and they feel too stiff for dancing. But somewhere between childish optimism and senile pessimism lies the youthful dance of hope, graceful in its stillness, since it knows how to wait in total attention for each new cue.

Waiting will be an expression of hope only when it is a "waiting for the Lord," for the God who is full of surprise—and for nothing else. As long as we wait for an improvement of the situation, our desires will make a great deal of noise. And if we wait for a deterioration of the situation, our fears will be noisy. The stillness that waits for the flash of the Lord's coming in any situation—that is the stillness of biblical hope. Not only is that stillness compatible with strenuous effort to change the situation, if that is our God-given task. It is only in that stillness that we shall clearly hear what our task is. How efficiently we go about that task will show itself again by stillness. After all, a machine that rattles squanders energy on the rattling. The stillness of hope is the expression of a perfect focusing of energy on the task at hand.

The stillness of hope is, therefore, the stillness of integrity. Hope integrates. It makes whole. And so, hope provides a sound basis for spiritual discipline, a solid mooring. (It is not by chance that the traditional emblem of hope is an anchor.) Remember for a moment how a talent for strong and healthy feelings can have an integrating effect on a person's inner life. Hope has a similar effect. But hope goes deeper and reaches further than mere feelings. It resonates through every part of a person's life, making it whole and sound.

It may be important for us to recognize the connection between hope and feelings—all the more so, since feelings are a neglected area in the main current of Christian spirituality. In fact, feelings have been viewed with suspicion for some time. At best, they have been given far less importance for our inner growth than intellect and will. This imbalance mirrors another significant imbalance.

Compared with all the stress on faith and love, relatively little stress has been put on hope. Only recently has hope been discovered, as it were, by spiritual writers. Could this double neglect of the virtue of hope and of feelings have something to do with the lack of inner wholeness, which many people painfully experience today?

We must distinguish, of course, between feelings and virtues. Hope is not merely a feeling. Hope is a virtue, a firmly established attitude of the heart, a basic bearing of the whole person. And yet we need only think of despair, the opposite of hope, to realize that feelings play an outstanding role in this area. Intellect, will, and emotions are all engaged in every virtue. The virtue of faith, for instance, characterizes every aspect of a faithful person's life. And yet here the cognitive power plays a predominant part. The virtue of love, as we shall see, transforms the whole person. Yet, at its core, love is an attitude of the will. In a similar way, the emotional aspect predominates in the virtue of hope, though intellect and will are certainly also affected. Neither intellect nor will should be misunderstood as if they were atomistic elements of our psyche. To misunderstand the emotions in this way would be almost impossible. It is so obvious how feelings always affect the whole person. This holistic quality of our feelings should help us understand how hope is a mark of spiritual wholeness.

The intellect perceives reality under the aspect

of truth. The will reaches out toward reality under the aspect of goodness. What appeals to our feelings is reality under the aspect of beauty. Our experience of beauty starts in our senses, but it goes beyond the sensuous. So do our feelings. Our whole being reverberates in response to that splendor of the real which we call beauty—so much so that for a moment we may feel ourselves transfigured by that radiance, which we behold not only before us, but within ourselves. Our intellect must labor for truth. Our will must struggle uphill toward goodness. But our feelings flow effortlessly toward beauty, with a graceful ease that reminds us again of the dancing stillness of hope.

There are other points where hope and beauty touch. One of these points is a paradox built into our attitude toward beauty, a paradox that sheds new light on hope. On the one hand, beauty always catches us by surprise. It always has the luster of a gift that is not only unexpected, but undeserved. Yet, on the other hand, we expect beauty. Deep in our heart we expect even our own beauty as a kind of inalienable birthright. Isn't that so?

> ... why is it
> we find the ugly unfair, not at all what the flesh
> was meant to be heir to, and as for beauty, assume
> a family right, as to an unforgettable heirloom?

Dorothy Donnelly asks this intriguing question in "Trio in a Mirror," a poem in which she explores the connection between beauty and hope. The answer she suggests is this:

> 'You are gods!' God said. But you are dark. A cloud
>   is on the star,
> And not a mirror in the world can show how
>   beautiful you are.

Hope can see what no mirror in the world can show. Hence,

> Happy fault, the flaw, which offending,
> lets us see we have eyes for the perfect. . . .

Our eyes for the perfect are the eyes of hope. Hope looks at all things the way a mother looks at her child, with a passion for the possible. But that way of looking is creative. It creates the space in which perfection can unfold. More than that, the eyes of hope look through all imperfections to the heart of all things and find it perfect.

The eyes of hope are grateful eyes. Before our eyes learned to look gratefully at the world, we expected to find beauty in good looking things. But grateful eyes expect the surprise of finding beauty in *all* things. And they do find it (remaining surprised). Goethe knew this when he wrote, late in his life:

> You fortunate eyes!
> Whatever you saw,

Whatever it was like,
How beautiful it was!

Before our hope was purified, we expected the best,
or at least the second or third best. But pure hope
expects the surprise that even the worst, if it happens, will be the best. And pure grateful hope is
never disappointed in this expectation.

I gave away the clue to this paradox by saying
that we are aware of it "deep in our heart." Our
innermost heart is that realm of full integration,
where we find our authentic identity: God's life
within us. There, faith is simply God's life as known
by heart-knowledge; that means known as faithfulness. And how does the heart perceive hope? Maybe
we could call hope God's life as felt by heart-feeling;
that means felt as beauty—expected and still surprising beauty—gracefulness. Imagine the gracefulness of a young prince, and you will see how birthright and surprise concur. At heart we are all
youthful princesses and princes. The spirit of hope is
a princely spirit. "Spiritus principalis," St. Jerome
called it in translating the verse "a steadfast spirit
renew within me" (Ps 51:10). The steadfastness of
hope is anchored in the heart.

If living from the heart means grateful living
and faithful living, it also means living full of hope.
Thus, hope gives fiber to our engagement in the
great concerns of our world today. We shall examine
this aspect of hope more closely.

Hope, as passion for the possible, gives us a

realistic alertness for practical possibilities. It gives us a youthfulness that sees the possible limited merely by an ever receding horizon. The princely spirit of hope initiates and determines our moral engagement. For it is rooted in the heart, where each of us is most intimately united with all others— and so responsible for all. Everything depends, of course, on how pure our hope is, how deeply it is rooted in the heart. There is ample room for self-deception here. So how can we check ourselves?

Maybe we could subject our hope to a simple test. It's not a foolproof test. Nor is it very precise. But it may give us a clue. You may want to try it out on one of your pet projects. First list the various hopes you have in view of that particular project. That's step one. Next, use your imagination to picture every single one of those hopes going down the drain. You may want to dwell on that possibility just long enough to feel the degree of despair to which it would tempt you. The hope that is left after all your hopes are gone—that is pure hope, rooted in the heart.

We have made an important distinction here between hope and hopes. It parallels our earlier distinction between faith and beliefs. We saw that faith leads to beliefs, just as hope leads to hopes. Yet, faith does not depend on beliefs, nor does hope depend on hopes. We even saw that beliefs can get in the way of faith. In a similar sense, hopes can get in the way of hope, stop up and block pure hope's openness for surprise. It makes a world of difference where we put our weight—on those hopes out there ahead of us, or on "the hope that is within."

A person of hope will have a whole array of lively hopes. But those hopes do not tell us much. The showdown comes when all the hopes get shattered. Then, a person of hopes will get shattered with them. A person of hope, however, will be growing a new crop of hopes as soon as the storm is over.

Those little hopes look harmless enough at first sight. They may even look impressively altruistic: Is not everything done in the best interest of those whom we want to help? But sooner or later we discover that those others don't exactly share the hopes we have for them. Poor things, they don't know any better. And, human nature being what it is, we might find ourselves pursuing our hopes more vigorously than those for whom we have such high hopes would like. Parents have ruined their children's lives for the sake of the hopes they had for them. Spouses have ruined one another's lives on account of hopes they considered the best for each other. Great nations, our own included, have been known to pursue over the dead bodies of other peoples—millions of bodies, torn, mutilated, burnt to death—hopes those peoples should have had, according to our conviction, not their own.

Hopes do not hasten the coming of peace on earth. Only hope does. For we can all too easily get stuck in our hopes, but no one can get stuck in hope. Hope liberates—first from the bondage of hopes, then from every other bondage. Pure hope is so steadfastly anchored at the moorings of the heart that it can afford to hold its own hopes lightly. That is the way a mother holds her children, lightly, no matter how firmly she holds them—always ready to give them up so they can grow, yet never letting them down. Hope mothers her hopes. And hope's dearest child is peace.

Hope, as openness for a future that does not come later, fully understands the watchword of the Catholic Worker: "There is no way to peace; peace is the way." Hope brings forth peace because it is rooted in peace, rooted in the heart where we are already one with all others. Hope unites. Hopes differ and tend to divide us. But we are united "in one hope" (Eph 4:4). And this "we" includes all creatures, the whole universe. "The whole of creation groans in a common labor pain," as St. Paul sees it, "in hope" (Rom 8:21f). What all creation is mothering forth in this labor of hope is God's "glory," our common princely birthright, "to be revealed in us" (Rom 8:18). "In fact, the fondest dream of the universe is to catch a glimpse of real live sons and daughters of God," as Clarence Jordan renders this key passage of Romans in his delightful *Cotton Patch Version of Paul's Epistles.* That hope is universal. For, just as faithfulness is at the heart of all things, so is hope.

And yet, how realistic is this hope? Look around you. Listen. From every corner of the world rises the cry: Time is running out! Everywhere it is the

same: our wasteful greed lays this world waste; our
fearfulness stockpiles threats that threaten to bring
about what we most fear; our indifference fails to
act when we *ought* to care, and so we cripple our
own power to make a difference when at last we *do*
care. It is hard to believe, but every day of the year
one endangered species of plant or animal life is
forever lost. Extinct. In one day this world spends
more money on weapons than the United Nations
can scrape together in a whole year for the World
Food Fund. Every single day hunger kills as many
men, women, and children as if a city of fifty-seven
thousand inhabitants were wiped off the map.
Wastefulness, fearfulness, indifference are undoing
us fast. Time is running out.

Once we have faced these facts, will it help to
close our eyes again? A painful truth has gotten
under our eyelids. There is no cure, but to open the
eyes of our heart, the eyes of hope. Hope discovers
within that time which is running out a different
kind of time—"time not our time"—a time that is
coming to fullness. It is under the image of mother
and child that hope sees and celebrates in every
moment "the fullness of time" (Gal 4:4). Christmas
happened when the mother's time was "fulfilled"
(Lk 2:6) and she gave birth. Christmas happens
again, here and now, the moment we mother the
princely child within us. Mother and child—there is
the image that challenges greed, fearfulness and
indifference. Everywhere in the world, mothers
nourish; they have courage, they care. The mothers

of the world challenge us to give birth to "the glorious freedom of the children of God" (Rom 8:21) through hope.

Are there methods, models, techniques for dealing with our worldwide problems? We must find them soon. Nothing is more urgent. But maybe it all begins with a change of attitude, a switch of emphasis from hopes to hope. Maybe we must first become more motherly. That means facing the whole enormous task, finding one small thing we can do, and doing it with a mother's dedication. In this way, hope is "redeeming the time" (Eph 5:16). Hope makes the most of time, exhausts time's possibilities, even time's unsuspected dimensions. In time that grows old, hope sees time that is with child. At the very moment when time is running out hope allows the fullness of time to break in.

With a view to that fullness of time, that "day of God" dawning, first century Christians asked, "What kind of persons ought we to be?" And they gave a twofold answer: We ought to be "looking forward to the Day of God (and) hastening its arrival" (2 Pet 3:12). The looking forward is the alert vision of hope. The hastening of the Day's arrival is the alert action of hope. Like a mother who looks at her child with the heart vision of hope and does the one little thing needed here and now, the alertness of hope joins vision and action together. Thus, the action of hope springs from the vision of the Peaceable Kingdom that is already "within" us. Isn't this the way people like Pope John XXIII, Dorothy Day,

Martin Luther King, and Mother Teresa radiate what they already hold in hope? This gives them power. "In silence and hope shall be your strength" (Is 30:15).

Silence and hope. They do belong together. Only in the silence of hope can we find our deepest communion. "We are all one silence," says Thomas Merton, "and a diversity of voices." How can we keep our ears attuned to the silence of our common hope when the divergent voices of our hopes distract us? How can we tune in to their ultimate harmony, audible only to the ears of the heart? Only by being still. Only by nurturing in our heart a stillness that grows big enough to embrace even contradictory hopes, a stillness strong enough to go beyond all hopes in hope.

Bach's "St. Matthew's Passion" opens with an interplay between the two halves of a double choir answering one another. And just when the intricate interweaving of this exchange reaches a climax beyond which it seems impossible to go, a surprise element breaks in: a boys' choir is added, superimposing the *cantus firmus* on the continuing intense interaction between the other two choirs. There are now three different choirs plus the orchestra, each following its own musical line. The effect of this pattern, measured in decibels, is intense loudness. And yet, surprisingly, the impression a listener gets is one of moving stillness.

The biblical term for the polyphony of hopes in the music of hope is "glory." How often hope and glory occur together in the New Testament! For the early Church, the concept of divine "glory" provided the link between the vision of hope and its ultimate realization. No less than the leverage for transforming the world rests on this pivotal concept "glory." "Glory," as understood today—and that means mostly misunderstood—is a somewhat dusty concept, stored away in the attic of our religious vocabulary. Like "majesty" it suggests not much more than pomp and circumstance. It seems to have little relevance for responsible Christian living. Who would guess that the concept of divine glory once provided the link between the vision of hope and its ultimate realization? And yet, for the early Church the leverage for transforming the world pivoted on their understanding of God's glory.

If only we could recover a sense of what "enlightenment by the good news of the glory of Christ" (2 Cor 4:4) meant to the first Christians. We would realize why that enlightenment had power to transform the ancient world. We would see that it still has power to transform even the social structures of our own time. But we would also become aware how closely glory is related to beauty.

It seems that the English word "glory" does not suggest beauty strongly enough. J.I. Rodale's *Synonym Finder,* my trusty companion, lists no less than ninety-two synonyms for glory; the word beauty is not among them. In the New Testament concept of glory the Hebrew notion of "weight" (*ka-*

bod) and the Greek notion of "appearance" (*doxa*) came to be fused into one. We might get the idea, if we imagine a glorious occasion on which famous stars make a personal appearance and throw their weight around, as we say. Glory, in the biblical sense, is certainly more than that. It is the manifestation of God's powerful presence, the overwhelming appearance of "the God of glory" (Ps 29:3). Beauty is implicit in all that. God's glory in light, fire, cloud, rainbow, starry sky, conveys a sense of surpassing beauty. We should, now and then, read "beauty" when we see "glory" printed in our Bibles. This would lead us to a deeper understanding of this key term—all the more, if we keep in mind the connection between beauty and hope, that we have already discussed.

A famous line from Rilke's *Duino Elegies* expresses in contemporary language that commingling of resplendence and power, so characteristic for God's glory in the Bible:

> . . . for beauty's nothing
> But the beginning of terror we're still just able to
>   bear,
> And why we adore it so is because it serenely
> Disdains to destroy us. . . .

If we thus think of God's glory as fascinating aura of awe, we might rescue it from the realm of pompous ceremonial and associate it more correctly with

beauty. Let us remember, though, that we experience beauty as "shattering" not only in stormwind,
earthquake, and fire, but in "a small, still voice" (1
Kgs 19:12), say in the gracefulness of a fawn. We
catch sight of it there, slender, dark against the
freshly fallen snow, motionless—and we are "un-
done." We can still feel the trembling from such an
encounter with overwhelming beauty when St. John
writes: "We beheld his glory, glory as of an Only-
begotten of a Father" (Jn 1:14).

This vision of divine glory leads to action. Glory
becomes, therefore, the key term for an understanding of Christian apostleship as the early Church saw
it. We can convince ourselves of this by reading, for
example, the Second Letter to the Corinthians. All
the quotations of the next two paragraphs are taken
from that early document. The term glory is repeated well over a dozen times here. The essence, the
goal, and the method of Christian witness in the
world are clearly spelled out. And it all hinges on
glory.

First of all, what is our calling as Christians? It is
"a ministry of reconciliation" (5:18) through "the
good news of the glory of Christ, who is the likeness
of God" (4:4). And what is the goal of this ministry?
"That the abounding grace may overflow, through
the thanksgiving of many, to the glory of God"
(4:15). But "who is qualified?" (2:16) the apostle asks,
for this "ministry of justice abounding in glory"
(3:9). The answer is: "We, all of us" (3:18). "Our

qualification is from God" (3:5). And why? "Because God who commanded light to shine out of darkness has kindled a light in our hearts, to shine forth and make known his glory, as he revealed it in the features of Jesus Christ" (4:6).

But the decisive question is one of method. How is our mission to be accomplished? There we receive a one-verse answer, inexhaustible in its richness: "We, all of us, catching as in a mirror, face unveiled, the glory of the Lord, are being transformed into that same likeness from glory to glory" (3:18). In the two parts of this crucial verse two aspects of the one calling are set side by side: transforming vision and visionary transformation. The bond between those two is the divine glory revealed in Christ. He is "the image of God" (4:4) in whose likeness we were created. That is why all of us are able in faith to catch sight of him in the microcosmic mirror of our heart. But notice, the pattern for the transformation of macrocosm and microcosm is one and the same. Christ is also the primordial pattern for the whole universe, which is destined to mirror divine beauty in nature and in history.

Because the believers saw in Christ God's Word, God's Wisdom, God's very Image, they professed that "all things were created in him ... through him, and for him" (Col 1:16). In him— because he is the eternal prototype, "icon of the invisible God, firstborn of all creation" (Col 1:15). Through him—because he is "the splendor of

(God's) glory" (Heb 1:3) that "shines in the darkness" (Jn 1:5) when God speaks in the beginning,
"Let there be light!" (Gen 1:3). For (or toward)
him—because, as the image that creation bears is
being developed, like a photographic image in a
darkroom, the full splendor of divine "glory is about
to be revealed in us" (Rom 8:18). Already, every
human being is the "image and glory of God" (1 Cor
11:7). Our transformation "from glory to glory" (2
Cor 3:18) may be understood as an ever more splen-
did realization of God's will, "on earth, as it is in
heaven." The same process may be understood as an
ever more faithful cosmic mirroring of God's beauty.

Beauty transforms the beholder. Beauty is winning. It wins you over. Even goodness and truth will
not be fully convincing to the human heart unless
they are gifted with a gracefulness and ease that
makes them beautiful. Take any period in history.
Who is still convinced by the arguments of its politicians, its philosophers, even its theologians? But
think of the poets of the same period or listen to its
music. We take a dim view of the hopes that inspired the crusaders. But their hope inspired the
cathedrals and still shines from every arch, sill, and
coping stone. Beauty, even in its most limited realization, holds an unquestionable promise of illimit-
able fulfillment. When we contemplate, say, the
great rose window at Chartres, we simply know
what it means that "we rejoice in hope of the glory
of God" (Rom 5:2).

Beauty is useless, superfluous, like all great things in life. Is not the universe itself a totally superfluous firework of divine glory, and *therefore* so priceless? Useful things have a price. But who can assess the value of a poem in dollars and cents? Who can put a price tag on a kiss? If God's glory is really all that matters, then the totally useless is not to be relegated to moments of spare time once in a month of Sundays. We may have to learn that the useless deserves prime time. The superfluous comes first in the order of importance. The necessary will claim attention anyway. To acknowledge this truth might mean a far more drastic transformation by divine glory than we were prepared to undergo. It might turn our set of values topsy-turvy. When Jesus says, "Behold the lilies" (Mt 6:28), he is inviting each one of us to take beauty seriously in all its uselessness. What will this mean for our daily life?

For the aesthete looking at those lilies involves no risk. It will never lead him to a change of heart. He has developed a sterile way of looking; he takes pleasure, but he gives nothing in return, least of all, his heart. The moment we give our heart to this vision a surprise happens. We thought we were looking at the lilies, but suddenly the lilies were looking at us. Rilke captures that experience in his poem "Archaic Torso of Apollo." It takes him twelve lines and a half to make his readers feel that they are gazing at the sculpture, which he sets before them, rather than describes. They are all eyes. At that moment, suddenly, the poet turns the perspective clear around and says: "there is no place/that does not see you." And abruptly he closes the poem with, "You must change your life." The lily looks at you and every petal becomes a tongue that challenges you.

With this challenge begins the transformation of our world. Once we rise to the challenge and accept the risk, transformation takes hold of us. It begins with a change of heart and runs its course, all the way to the transformation of the social order and to the transformation of matter itself.

The aesthete is too jaded to run that risk. The do-gooder is too busy. He has no time to bother with flowers. With six tongues the glory of God shouts at us from every lily in bloom, "Stop and look!" Or, as the Psalm puts it, "Be still and know" (Ps 46:10). But the busybody does not understand the language of their silent eloquence. He rushes on: "Sorry, I don't speak Lily." His ears are buzzing with the din of his own projects, ideas, and good intentions.

While the aesthete in us falls into the trap of barren vision, the do-gooder in us is trapped in barren action. Over against both of them stands the person of hope, with clear eyes and rolled-up sleeves. Hope is the virtue that frees us from the double trap of idle vision and blind action. The aesthete and the busybody are desperate in opposite ways. The one despairs of the power of action and gets drunk on vision. The other drowns his despair of finding a guiding vision in mere activity. But hope brings us right back to the core of contemplative transformation: glory.

Glory is seed and harvest of hope, its initial spark and its ultimate blaze. When the first Christians tried to sum up "the good news, proclaimed now to every creature under heaven," hope and glory were indispensable key words. When they attempted to bring into one formula "the secret hidden from ages and generations, but now made manifest," this is what they came up with: "Christ in you, the hope of glory" (Col 1:23–27). They speak of it as God's "secret among the nations," a divine master plan, if you wish, for social transformation. But this "hope of glory" is more than a secret blueprint. It is "hidden" like leaven in the dough. And the apostle speaks of it as "that energy of His, which is at work in me with power" (Col 1:29).

Giving yourself to the transforming power of "Christ within you" implies self-acceptance. God has accepted you—as you are—because God looks at your heart of hearts and sees His own glory—Christ—reflected as in a mirror. To accept God's acceptance of us makes self-acceptance possible. To accept God's acceptance is also the basic gesture of faith, our trust in the Giver, from whom we receive all, even ourselves. And to accept God's acceptance is also the basic gesture of hope, our openness for Surprise, including all the surprises of our own unsuspected possibilities. The Self of this self-acceptance is "Christ within." In *Four Quartets*, T.S. Eliot calls it:

> A condition of complete simplicity
> (Costing not less than everything)
> And all shall be well and
> All manner of thing shall be well.

But before all manner of things shall be well, the most painful test of hope still awaits us. We have to face that test when the one hope of our common calling (cf. Eph 4:4) gives rise to mutually conflicting hopes within the one Body of Christ. An example is the tension among our sisters and brothers in Latin America today, where hope, hopes, and social transformation are at stake. "It is necessary," says St. Paul, "that there should be factions among you, so that the approval may become apparent" (1 Cor 11:19). Our limited visions give rise to limited hopes. And those hopes must clash with each other so that God's surpassing plan may emerge. That is why we must hold our hopes lightly at the same time as we are willing to die for them. There is no greater suffering than that. Yet, suffering gives weight, that weight without which glory is just flimsy glitter.

When hopes clash with hopes for the sake of the one surpassing hope, it becomes clear in what sense we "glory in the cross of our Lord Jesus Christ" (Gal 6:14). We glory in it not as in a jewel-studded emblem of triumph, but as in each one's own, most unprepossessing suffering—Martin Luther King's, Karen Silkwood's, Oscar Romero's, your own. The trajectory of hope is not an unbroken line "from glory to glory." It leads through the paradox of the cross. The cross itself is a sign of contradiction. Its two lines meet in conflict, like clashing hopes. The cross stands for that collision in which our hopes must go down so that on the third day hope may rise. The risen Lord says to his discouraged disciples: "Was it not necessary for the Christ to suffer all this and so to enter into His glory?" (Lk 24:26).

"Hail, holy cross, one only hope," sings an ancient Christian hymn. "O crux ave, spes unica!" Why should the cross be an emblem of hope rather than hopelessness? All Jesus' hopes were shattered when he hung on the cross. Why was it "necessary" for the Christ to suffer all this? We set our hopes on what we can imagine. But hope is open for the unimaginable. "No eye has seen, no ear has heard, what God has prepared" for us. That is why our desperate little hopes must be crossed out to make room for the surpassing Surprise, "the God of hope," whose breaking into our lives is death and resurrection.

A friend who read the manuscript for me wrote in the margin at this point: "Give life experience example." A well meant advice, but an impossible task. No life experience can exemplify God's breaking in, for that event is a death experience. Its other side is resurrection. But resurrection is not revival, survival, resuscitation. Resurrection is not a coming back to this life of death. What would be the point of that? Resurrection is a going forward into death and

through death into a fullness that lies beyond life
and death as we know them. From this side of the
great divide, death remains all we can see, unless
we are looking at some mirage of hopes. Hope looks
squarely at death, the open door for Surprise.

On Easter morning the angel announces the
resurrection of Jesus not by saying, "Here he is; he
has come back to life!" No. Looking for him in that
way would mean looking for the living one among
the dead. He is not here. Nor is he alive with our
aliveness that is closer to death than to life. "He is
risen," runs the good news, and "He is not here." All
we can experience from the perspective of our
deathbound living is that the tomb is open and
empty, a fitting image for wide open hope.

Hope shares the ambiguity of Jesus' cross. Hope
is a passion for the possible. The double meaning of
the word "passion" takes on a new significance in
the light of Christ's cross. Hope, as passion for the
possible, implies passionate dedication to the possible as well as suffering for its realization. Only patience fulfills this double task. A mother's patience is
the passion of hope. And since patience is as conta-
gious as impatience, it will also be our way of
strengthening each other's hope. But it will demand
from us a passion for—and for the sake of—goals,
yes, even hopes, for which one might have to give
one's life without getting attached to them.

The unattached devotion which might pass for
devotionless, in a drifting boat with a slow leakage.

The slow leakage T.S. Eliot describes comes from the fact that for our hopes, which move in time, time is running out. But for hope, which "abideth," time is filling up toward the fullness of time, here and now.

> Here the impossible union
> Of spheres of existence is actual,
> . . .
> For most of us, this is the aim
> Never here to be realized;
> Who are only undefeated
> Because we have gone on trying.

Most of us are so used to an overabundance of words that silence tends to frighten us. It seems to us like a vast empty space. We look down into its expanse and get dizzy. Or else we feel a marvelous attraction toward the silence that leaves us bewildered. "I don't know what has happened to me," someone says. "I used to feel comfortable with my prayers, but lately I just want to be there in God's presence. I don't feel like saying or doing or thinking anything at all in prayer. And even God's presence is more like an absence of all that I can imagine. There must be something wrong with me!" Wrong? I do not think so. This silence, too, is gift of God. And if we own it as the expression of our openness for surprise, we discover that this great emptiness of hope is already filled to the brim with the unimaginable.

This must be paradoxical, because it brings us back to the paradox of God's life within us, the starting point of this chapter on hope. At the silent center of our heart, the fullness of life strikes us as a great emptiness. It must be so. For that fullness surpasses what eye has seen and ear has heard. Only gratefulness, in the form of limitless openness for surprise, lays hold of the fullness of life in hope.

Love: A "Yes" to Belonging

In the two preceding chapters we have seen that faith and hope are always there when one is grateful. We saw that one must have trust in the giver before one can give thanks. But trust of this kind is the very core of faith. And we recognized also that one must be open for surprise before one can be grateful. Deep down, every gift is a surprise. But openness for surprise is the essence of hope. Faith and hope, in this sense, are two aspects of the divine life within us. The third one, often mentioned in the same breath, is love. It, too, is intimately tied in with giving thanks. The ties between love and gratefulness are what we shall explore in this chapter.

In getting at the roots of faith and hope, we had to use a trick, which we shall use here, too. We had to carefully distinguish faith and hope from their popular misconceptions. It would be all too easy, as we saw, to confuse faith with beliefs and hope with hopes. Yet, this would lead us, in the long run, far astray. We tend to assume that we know the mean-

163

ing of basic concepts like faith, hope, or love. But,
precisely because they are so basic, we need to re-
examine now and then what they really mean.
When the roof of our house is leaking, everyone
notices it. When a window pane is broken, the dam-
age is obvious. We can fix it before greater harm
happens. But when the foundation walls begin to
shift, we are in trouble. We may not be aware of it
until it is too late. Even a slight shift can, in time,
cause the whole building to topple.

The conceptual shifts we detected are slight,
indeed. But they are consequential. It is a minute
shift of emphasis from hope to hopes, from believing
in someone to believing something. Yet, we saw that
hopes can in the end get in the way of hope, and
beliefs can become obstacles to faith, when we cling
to them. When we look closely, we discover that a
similar change of emphasis has taken place in our
general understanding of love. In fact, the problem
here is every bit as dangerous, if not more so, for it is
more difficult to discern. What has happened to our
understanding of love? What shift has happened to
this basic concept?

We can get an inkling of the problem when we
focus on the difficulty that most of us experience
with the command to love our enemies. Remember,
everything in this book must be able to stand the
test of your own experience. What I propose remains a mere suggestion until it is validated by your
experience. If your own experience doesn't bear it
out, it is not true—not true for you, at any rate. In

case you never had any difficulty loving your enemies, my argument will be lost on you. For most of
us, however, the problem will be a real one. Merely
thinking about loving our enemies, we get already
entangled in contradictions. Love, in the sense we
normally give to that word, is simply not applicable
to enemies.

Normally, we have preference and desire in
mind when we speak of love. For most of us, love, in
the full sense, is a passionate attraction. Given this
notion of love, we need not put it to the extreme
test of loving our enemies. Loving our neighbors up
and down the street with a passionate attraction is
sufficiently grotesque a notion. Even long before we
get to the Bible, we find that there must be something wrong with thinking of love as preferential
desire. This notion applies, in fact, only to a small
number of the many cases in which we speak of
love. Where it fits most obviously is in the case of
lovers. Beyond that, things get problematic.

Even for lovers the current notion of love becomes less applicable to their relationship the more
their love matures. Preference grows less and less
exclusive; desire finds fulfillment in mutual belonging; and yet, their love keeps growing. But if love as
preferential desire fits even in the most typical case
only in a measure, what shall we say of other examples? Do we love our parents with a passionate
attraction? And yet, we do love them. The word
"love" is surely appropriate among brothers and
sisters. But do we mean desire when we use it?

Obviously, there must be something askew with the current notion of love.

What is it that has gone wrong? Why do we give so narrow a meaning to the word "love" that it fits only a fraction of the cases in which we actually use it? I have a theory that explains—to my own satisfaction at least—how this narrowing of the notion of love comes about. Long before we begin to reflect on love, long before we even learn to speak, we do love. We love our parents, our playmates, our pets, our toys. Passionate attraction is hardly what characterizes any of these relationships. Nor does anyone take much notice of that love. It is like the air we breathe. But then, let's say in kindergarten, we fall in love. This, now, is passionate attraction, at least in miniature. And suddenly everybody makes a big ado about this puppy love. Our little classmates giggle and tease us and write on the wall "Johnny loves Betsy." And the adults smile and call it our first love, as if we hadn't known love before. It's no wonder that this experience so impresses us that this one form of love becomes in our minds the norm for every other form, whether it will fit or not.

If preferential desire is far too narrow a notion of love, what is a more adequate one? If it is to apply in all cases, it ought to apply also to Johnny's puppy love. We should be able, therefore, to find in his experience—and in our own, if our memory is good enough—an element that characterizes love in all its forms. What is that element? It certainly is overshadowed by the passionate attraction that strikes us most. But underneath is something different: a sudden experience of belonging to Betsy, which Johnny accepts with delight. So overwhelming is this sense of belonging, in fact, that it spills over, as it were. Those of us who grew up in a big family may remember that we could tell right away when one of our brothers or sisters had fallen in love. But how? They were suddenly so kind to everybody in the family. Johnny washes the dishes and doesn't forget to take out the garbage when his turn comes. That's a dead giveaway: he's in love. And why does he do so? Because his sense of belonging is aroused and his joyful acceptance of belonging to another spills over, even to his family, whom he normally takes for granted. We shall find this "yes" to belonging in every form love takes.

It would be an endless task to prove this point by running through every conceivable case of love in order to show that both a sense of belonging and a willing "yes" to that belonging is implied. But there is an easier way. We may be able to agree that the opposite of love is indifference, rather than hatred. Experience proves, in fact, that we find it hard to tell, at times, whether we love or hate someone. But this is never someone toward whom we are indifferent. Indifference is a clear-cut "no" to belonging. Both love and hatred do care. Indifference says: "I don't care. I have nothing to do with this one." It stands to reason, then, that a "yes" to belonging should be a universal characteristic of love as diametrically opposed to indifference.

We can test this understanding of love against the precept to love our enemies. Now things look different. The notion of romantic love just wouldn't fit. But we and our enemies certainly belong together—obviously not in the same way as friends belong together, but it is a belonging, nevertheless. Moreover, by choosing our friends, we choose our enemies. If we have no enemies, maybe we have never had the courage to take sides. The command to love our enemies implies that we must have enemies. How else could we love them? God certainly has enemies. "As it is written: Jacob have I loved and Esau have I hated" (Mal 1:2f; Rom 9:13). Yet, the same God is love. When the psalmist makes God's enemies his own, he sings: "I hate them with a perfect hatred" (Ps 139:22). Perfect hatred may treat enemies with outrage, with determination, even with cunning. But it will always treat them with patience, with respect, with fairness. Perfect hatred cares. It will cultivate all possible lines of communication with the enemy. If we could purge the word "hatred" of any connotation of indifference we could put it this way: perfect hatred is loving hatred. It opposes its enemies clearly and strongly, but it never forgets to affirm: we belong together. Whatever I do to you, I do it ultimately to myself.

It is the concept of self that expands when we come to understand what love really means. The current idea of love identifies our self with our little individualistic ego. This little ego translates "Love thy neighbor as thyself" into a series of incredible mental acrobatics. Step one: imagine you are someone else. Step two: try to whip up a passionate attraction for that imaginary other. Step three: try to feel for someone who is really someone else the same passionate attraction you felt for yourself (if you did) when you were imagining that you were someone else. That's asking a little much, isn't it? And yet, the command is so simple: "Love your neighbor as (being) yourself." That means: realize that your self is not limited to your little ego. Your true self includes your neighbor. You belong together—radically so. If you know what self means, you know what belonging means. It costs you no effort to belong to yourself. Spontaneously, you say "yes" to yourself in your heart. But at heart you are one with all others. Your heart knows that your true self includes your neighbor. Love means that you say "yes" from your heart to that true self—and act accordingly.

Belonging is always mutual. This is true even in the case of things that belong to us. We tend to think of our relationship to belongings as a one-sided proprietorship. This colors our love for things. It gives it the wrong color. Rightly understood, love for things, too, is a "yes" to belonging—to a mutual belonging, whether or not we are aware of this. You may think your car belongs to you merely in the sense of being your property, serving your needs. But the car knows better. She won't serve your needs for long, unless you serve her needs in turn and have her serviced. It's mutual: "I'll take you there, if you keep my oil level up." If you really love your car, you'll be sensitive to her needs. You will intuitively understand that the two of you belong together. Love takes that mutual belonging seriously. Love cares, even for things.

Mutual belonging has, of course, degrees of depth and intimacy. On the level of things it is least demanding and most easily dissolved. My Swiss army knife makes very few demands on me for the excellent service it provides. And if I should lose it, anyone who finds it would quickly be able to become its happy owner. The plants I have raised may not so easily take to someone else. And when it comes to lost pets, we realize that we are dealing with a far more intense level of mutual belonging. It may be hard to tell who feels the loss more deeply, the one who lost a dog or the lost dog. My little niece sent a picture postcard from vacation to her poodle and signed it "Lisa, Your Owner." The poodle, however, leaves no doubt about considering herself Lisa's owner, like the pig in Denise Levatow's delightful poems, who speaks of the family as "my humans."

Among humans, mutual belonging can obviously reach an intensity far beyond anything we experience in our relationship to things, plants, or animals. It is here that we speak most properly of love. Some people would, in fact, insist that the English word "love" should be restricted to human beings and to

God. But I have made an observation. Among my
acquaintances, the people who are most pedantic
about the grammatical distinction between loving
and liking tend to be the ones who are least sensitive to the fact that belonging is always mutual to
some degree. The same people often find it difficult
to think of our relationship to God as genuinely
mutual.

I must admit that, for a long time, I myself
found it somewhat presumptuous to address God in
prayer as "my" God. At that time, ownership was
the main meaning I gave to "my" and "mine." And
ownership meant to me the right of possession, with
no thought of the duties that go with the right.
Gradually, however, I came to see that I myself
somehow belong to everything that belongs to me,
that belonging implies a give-and-take. Maybe this
insight came to me when I discovered that the
tomato plants in my corner of the garden would wilt
when I forgot to give them water; that my white
mouse insisted on being fed, or else she would nib-
ble on things I didn't want to give her; that even my
roller skates demanded a certain care from me. I
discovered also something else: things belong more
to me, the more I belong to them. The little word
"my" means more when it refers to my pet turtle
than when it refers to my shoes, and more still when
it refers to the group of friends to whom I belong. If
I belong most of all to God, it follows that God
belongs more fully to me than anything else I could

call my own. In fact, I have since come to realize that the only time when "my" rings really true is when one says "my God."

This tells me something new about the word "my." It shows me that "my" is most appropriately used when its meaning is least exclusive. Let me put it differently: the more something is truly mine, the less it is exclusively mine. We realize this in those moments when we are most awake, most alive, in moments when we get an inkling of God. In those moments we experience total belonging. We simply know for a moment that all belongs to us, because we belong to all. In the light of that experience we can say from our heart, "All is mine." But "mine" is not the least bit exclusive. It comes from the heart, where each is one with all. The heart says "yes" to this universal belonging and knows at once that "Yes" is a name of God. For me, this sheds new light on the truth that "God is love" (Jn 4:8).

The moments in which we experience this are key moments for understanding what fullness of life means. That is why we have to refer to them time and again. They are also moments of overwhelming gratefulness. We have seen this before, but now we are in a better position to understand why this is so. At the very beginning of our investigation of gratefulness we discovered: the turning point between receiving a gift and giving thanks is the "yes" to the interdependence between giver and receiver. Gift-giving and thanks-giving turn on the pivot of this "yes." Giver and receiver belong together in thanksgiving. And the "yes" to this belonging is no other but the "yes" of love. We have seen how difficult it is at times to say the "yes" of gratitude in our daily life. But in moments when our heart beats high with aliveness, we experience the interdependence of all with all as freedom, as joy, as fulfillment. Our heart catches a glimpse of home, and home is where all depend on all. No wonder that a "yes" springs from our heart like a long sigh of relief, of liberation, of homecoming. It is like being in love with the whole universe.

In love? Here we come back to Johnny and Betsy, to the experience of falling in love. Now we see what falling in love is meant to do for us in life's plan. It is to open our eyes. Love makes blind, one says. True enough. A pleasantly selective blindness strikes us when we fall in love. But in a different respect love opens our eyes. We suddenly see the bliss of belonging. And, deep down, that sense of belonging is all-embracing. On the surface, it may focus only on the limited object of our infatuation, that charming creature with freckles. But it is as if a window had been opened onto one little corner of a wide landscape. This is a start. If we keep looking, we will sooner or later discover a whole new world. By exploring what we glimpsed when we fell in love, we will grow in love, in gratitude, and so in aliveness.

Growing in love means drawing out the implications of that "yes" which our heart sings out spontaneously when we are at our best. But drawing out these implications is not an easy task. Falling in love happens by itself; rising to the heights of love costs an effort. It demands no less determination, attention, and precision than the soaring spirals of the Windhover, the "falcon, in his riding," that stirred Gerard Manley Hopkins to one of his finest poems. Rising in love demands precision and attention, because we must be ready, moment by moment, to face unforeseen implications of our "yes" and to quickly make the right response. It demands determination to rebuff the big wind, to bridle up when indifference threatens to overpower us. Falling in love is barely the beginning of a great love. The glimpses we catch of our great, blissful belonging are merely a challenge to growth in relationships, a challenge to grow to our full human stature. Only on the wings of love will we rise to that challenge.

The image of a great bird soaring on wide wings suggests the stillness of a fully dedicated will. When Christian tradition speaks of love, the accent falls on our human will, not on our emotions. This is another indication that the notion of passionate attraction is far off the mark when we search for the essence of love. Love is not a feeling, but a freely chosen attitude. Only so does the command "Thou shalt love" make sense. No one can command us to feel one way or another. Feelings are simply not subject to commands. Neither are our thoughts. Only our will can obey. As our will makes a vigorous effort to overcome the inertia of indifference, it will take our thoughts and our feelings along step by step.

"Thou shalt love" is a command that calls for three steps: first, saying "yes" to belonging; next, to look and see what our "yes" implies; finally, to act upon that "yes." One step leads to the next. If we have said the first "yes" with full conviction, we will surely care enough about those to whom we belong to inform ourselves about them. This includes exploited brothers and sisters at home and abroad. (We might even discover that we are among those who exploit them.) It includes the sea otters and the whales. It includes the rain forests. "Thou shalt love" implies all the effort it takes to find out what I personally can do to act upon my "yes" to belonging in a given case. And, little as it may be, there is always something I can do. Most importantly, therefore, "Thou shalt love" implies that I go ahead and do what I can, because I belong and have said "Yes, I will."

This response of love is a grateful response. Here, too, love and gratefulness meet. When love acts upon the implications of its "yes" to belonging, there is no mistaking its response for the rushing-about of do-gooders who expect thanks for their service. Here the service itself is an expression of our thanks for the opportunity to serve. It springs from a deep inner listening, an openness for all that a given moment contains, because we belong to it all, and so we care. Every moment is gift. We have seen this before. But now we must stress that the gift within each gift is opportunity. It may be opportunity to enjoy; it may be opportunity to patiently accept what cannot be changed; but it may also be opportunity to get up and do something about it. "On strong wings love rises to every opportunity and so shows itself grateful for it." If we miss this point, gratitude becomes a passive, bloodless affair. But if we look at every moment as an opportunity to say again and anew the "yes" of love with all its implications, then love will be seen as a power that can change the world. Yet, love will change the lover first.

We grow in love when we grow in gratefulness. And we grow in gratefulness when we grow in love. Here is the link between the two: thanksgiving pivots on our willingness to go beyond our independence and to accept the give-and-take between giver and thanks-giver. But the "yes" which acknowledges our interdependence is the very "yes" to belonging, the "yes" of love. Every time we say a simple "thank you," and mean it, we practice that inner gesture of "yes." And the more we practice it, the easier it becomes. The more difficult it is to say a grateful "yes," the more we grow by learning to say it gracefully. This sheds light on suffering and on other difficult gifts. The hardest gifts are, in a sense, the best, because they make us grow the most.

We know that our deepest joy springs from living in love. The key to that joy is the "yes" which love and gratefulness have in common. Thanksgiving is the setting in which that "yes" is most naturally practiced. This makes gratefulness a school in which one learns love. The only degrees one receives in that school are degrees of aliveness. With every "yes," one relationship or another grows deeper and broader. And aliveness can only be measured by the intensity, depth, and variety of our relationships. If the fullness of gratitude which the word grate-ful-ness implies can ever be reached, it must be fullness of love and fullness of life.

Growth in grateful love is also growth in prayer. Love has its own world of prayer, just as faith and hope do. We saw that faith ventures forth into a world of prayer, whose countless forms are so many ways of "Living by the Word." Hope opens itself in the stillness of waiting to a world of prayer that is still at the brink of beginning, still open for untold possibilities, the Prayer of Silence. Love belongs to a world of prayer at the intersection of Word and Silence. Love's prayer is action. The Word, received in faith, falls as seed into the silent soil of hope and brings fruit in love. There is no willfulness in love's action, only a willingness to bear fruit. And yet the active aspect is so striking here that love's world of prayer goes by the name of Contemplation in Action.

This name will strike us as strange if we remember our chapter on contemplation. Action is a constituent part of contemplation, one of its two poles. The other pole is vision. The "con" in contemplation welds vision and action together. Unless action put it into effect, vision would remain barren in this world. The opposite of Contemplation in Action cannot be inactive contemplation. That would be as

contradictory as blind contemplation. Action belongs as much to contemplation as vision. Why,
then, single it out when we speak of Contemplation
in Action? Here is an explanation. In love's world of
prayer, action does not only flow from contemplative vision, but that very vision flows also from contemplative action. Here is a parallel from daily experience. Sometimes you want to do something, but
you say, "I don't see how it can be done." Then you
try it anyway, and the doing shows you how. "I see!"
you exclaim. Thus, vision can spring from action,
even the vision of God's glory.

Every genuine form of contemplation is committed to putting its vision into action. But not always does the vision spring from active engagement
itself. Often our vision quest demands that we disengage ourselves from activity. For love's world of
prayer, however, the intense engagement of Contemplation in Action is most typical. This does not
mean that contemplative disengagement is inactive
or lacking in love. Not at all. But the "yes" to belonging makes love what it is. And that "yes" implies availability for engagement. Thus, love is most
easily recognized in contemplation, the more the
engagement aspect is stressed. Suppose you want to
draw a picture of a pencil. You will most likely make
two parallel lines and add a point in front. But you
could just as well draw a small circle with a dot in
the center. That's a front view of a pencil. Front
view and side view show the same thing. But one is

far more easily recognized. That is why we speak of Contemplation in Action as love's world of prayer. Love is most easily recognized in it.

Let us make sure we mean what we say: Contemplation *in* Action, not contemplation *during* action. This may be a fine point, but it will help us define still more clearly what we mean. My mother knits all kinds of sweaters for her children and grandchildren and for her great-grandchild. And while she is doing so, she likes to pray the rosary. Now, that is contemplation *during* action. During her knitting, my mother savors God's faithfulness, mystery by mystery, and her faith is nourished by that food. She enters the world of prayer most typical of faith. We called it Living by the Word. But she is also entering love's world of prayer, simply by knitting lovingly, in spite of the arthritic pain in her fingers. By doing so she understands God's love more and more deeply in and through her own action. This is Contemplation *in* Action, a way of coming to know God's love from within by acting it out.

This example happens to show, by the way, that the worlds of prayer include each other. Prayer is prayer. What matters is that we pray, not that we can label our prayer with precision. At times, however, it can be helpful to know how to tell the different worlds of prayer apart. Some men and women are true contemplatives without knowing it. In the midst of busy lives they are practicing Con-

templation in Action. Yet they are hankering for
forms that belong to a different world of prayer,
instead of growing more at home in the one in
which they do live.

A school teacher, for instance, comes home exhausted from having taken her class to the zoo.
"And all day long I didn't have a minute to pray,"
she complains. Well chances are she did nothing *but*
pray all day long. Her heart was steeped in Contemplation in Action, and her head doesn't even recognize it. The love that made her care for each child
with full attention was God's love flowing through
her. By savoring this love from within, she could
have a whole day of prayer—and prayer without
distraction at that. She can't risk being distracted
from her attention to the children. But this single-
minded attention is, in this case, her prayerful attention to God, if she gives her heart to it.

"But what if I'm not even thinking of God?"
someone will ask. "Can this still be prayer?" Well,
are you still breathing, even though you are not
thinking of the air you breathe? Action is realized by
acting, not by thinking about it. And Contemplation
in Action is that contemplation in which we realize
God by acting in love. Thinking about God is important. But acting in God leads to a deeper knowledge.
Lovers are closer to love than scholars who merely
reflect on love. It would be a bit awkward to reflect
on kissing while you kiss.

During a simple action like knitting—simple for

my mother, not for me—one can think about God and still do the work well. If your job is typing, it will be more difficult to contemplate during that action. The Governor may find himself addressed as Godernor, but apart from typing errors little harm will result. A teacher, however, taking twenty-two children to the zoo, better not try contemplation during that action. She might come home minus one youngster. Her only choice is Contemplation *in* Action, or none at all. And what a joyful surprise to discover that she can find God in, not only during, her loving service. No one is barred by outward circumstances from a life of contemplation. Many people struggle to make extremely active lives more prayerful. The discovery of Contemplation in Action can bring them great relief and great encouragement.

There is also a trap hidden here. Our activities create something like a centrifugal force. They tend to pull us from our center into peripheral concerns. And the faster the spin of our daily round of activities, the stronger that pull. We need to counteract it by anchoring ourselves in the silent center of our heart. "My work is my prayer," someone says. Well, it had better be! After all, we are to "pray at all times." Work should not make us stop praying. But when my work becomes my only prayer, it won't be prayer much longer. Its weight will pull me off-center. We can hear it quickly when a clothes dryer spins unevenly. Why can't we hear it when our lives do the same? It may be time to stop and reload. It may be time for nothing-but-prayer, time to disengage ourselves, to find our center, and to re-engage ourselves from the heart. Then our work will truly be prayer. It will be Contemplation in Action.

Shaker tradition has a saying that puts the idea of contemplation as simply as it can be put: "Hearts to God, hands to work." That is how Shakers lived. We need only to look at a Shaker chair for proof that they understood contemplation. "Hearts to God" means attention to the guiding vision. "Hands to work" means making that vision a reality. The inseparable splicing of vision and action makes contemplation what it is. In love's world of prayer, the vision is a deep awareness of belonging; the action puts the consequences of that belonging into practice. Love's action is an expression of thanksgiving for the insights of love's vision. This is what the Romans called "gratias agere," not merely thanking, but acting out one's gratefulness. With a heart turned to God, love sees: I belong. With hands turned to work, love acts accordingly.

The Romans had a word for love, which expressed precisely that attitude. It is the Latin word *pietas.* We could translate it as "family affection," an attitude that springs from a sense of belonging and expresses itself in acting accordingly. *Pietas* is, in the first place, the attitude of the *pater familias.* The family belongs to the father from whom it receives its name. *Pietas* gives rights and duties to the *pius pater.* But *pietas* is an attitude shared by every member of the household and relating each to each. Husband and wife may love one another with passion and desire, but the bond that holds them most strongly and most deeply together is *pietas.* So is the love of brothers and sisters for each other and the love between children and parents. But *pietas* extends also to servants and slaves, to anyone who belongs to the household. As a household they are related to the ancestors of the family and to the guardian spirits, the *lares,* by the same *pietas* that embraces the household pets, the farm animals, the land, the tools, the furniture, and other heirlooms. We have no concept like that in English. If we could put the vigor of the Latin *pietas* into our words "pity" and "piety," which derive from it, our concepts of compassion and devotion would surely be enriched. They hinge on the notion of belonging. We cannot revive a word at will. But we must recover the sense of belonging that coined the word *pietas.*

It is fascinating to trace the process by which archaic societies make a stranger welcome. It teaches us much about love, about belonging, and about gratitude. An outsider is strange in the sense of being unfamiliar, if not belonging to the family. But what is unfamiliar is strange also in the sense of being suspicious. The stranger is suspect of being an enemy. Being aware of this suspicion, a stranger with good intentions will carry gifts. They are not a price to be paid but a free present. Will they be accepted? If so, the give-and-take of gratitude forges a bond of mutual belonging. The one who was a stranger is now a guest. And guests belong to the household. In their regard the bond of *pietas* has a special sacredness. When we become aware that every stranger *is* gift, strangers need no longer go through a gift-giving ritual to be accepted. We will welcome them, and this hospitality of the heart will be a celebration of the bond that unites giver and receiver in thanksgiving.

When we lift our hearts to God, whom we call "Our Father in heaven," we see that we belong to a household that embraces all creatures, the Earth Household in Gary Snyder's powerful poetic term. And if we put our hands to work in service of that Earth Household, this contemplative matching of vision by action will spread God's peace "on earth as it is in heaven." The crucial question is: How big is our family? How wide is the reach of our belonging? Can we stretch it to the furthest reaches of God's household? Will our care and concern stretch to embrace all members of this Earth Household— humans, animals, plants, whom we now still consider strange? The survival of all of us may well depend on our answer.

Peace is the fruit of love. The "yes" to our belonging to God's great household is the seed from which peace unfolds. D.H. Lawrence suggests this in a poem which he entitled "PAX," the Latin word for "peace." There is a close link between the Ro-

man concepts of *pax* and *pietas*. This poem hinges
on the link between the two.

> All that matters is to be at one with the living God
> To be a creature in the house of the God of Life.

> Like a cat asleep on a chair
> at peace, in peace
> and at one with the master of the house, with the
>   mistress,
> at home, at home in the house of the living,
>   sleeping on the hearth, and yawning before the
>   fire.

> Sleeping on the hearth of the living world,
> yawning at home before the fire of life
> feeling the presence of the living God
> like a great reassurance
> a deep calm in the heart
> a presence
> as of a master sitting at the board
> in his own and greater being,
> in the house of life.

When we read this poem aloud, it has the power of an incantation. Its repetitions seem to put us
under a spell—not a spell that binds us, but a freeing
spell. "At one . . . at peace, in peace and at one . . . at
home, at home . . . at home." This incantation makes
us relax. It makes us settle down into "a deep calm
in the heart." It is like a homecoming to "the house

of life," to "the house of the living," to "the house of the God of life," where we belong, where we are truly at home. In all their calm, these lines are alive with dynamic power. They have fire in them. Even the yawning of the cat is a "yawning before the fire." The yawning of any self-respecting cat is part of a whole ritual of stretching and arching that is full of vitality. When we yawn not with boredom or fatigue but with "a deep calm in the heart," it is a "yawning before the fire of life." "Life" is a key word in this poem. Five times "life" and "living" are repeated. The calm of true peace is not a dead silence but the live stillness of a bright burning flame.

"All that matters," absolutely all, "is to be at one with the living God." And "the God of life" is present in "the house of life" as "the fire of life." (Placed at the beginning, middle, and end of the poem, these three phrases are given prominence.) Fire is often an image of love. But here it is not the raging and consuming fire of passion. It is the calm, life-giving fire on the hearth that makes everyone in the house feel welcome and at home. How are we, then, "to be at one with the living God," if this is all that matters? By allowing that hearth fire to warm us to the bone; by letting that warmth make us feel at home; by simply being "at home, at home in the house of the living." There is no split between heaven and earth in a world warmed by love." The house of life "is" the house of the God of life.

God's presence in the Earth Household is

a presence
as of a master sitting at the board
in his own and greater being,
in the house of life.

The image of the *pater familias* gives meaning to
these lines and protects them at the same time from
a pantheistic misunderstanding. The world is no
more one with God than the household is one "with
the master of the house, with the mistress." No
more, but no less either. It is not a matter of being
one, but "at one," through that love which only the
notion of *pietas* can begin to convey. Yet, what
reverence it inspires to be aware of this at-one-ness.
If we think of the Earth Household as our heavenly
Father's "own and greater being," this will make us
look at every pebble, every burr, every wood louse
with reverence—and act accordingly. It will cause
love to take its likes and dislikes as lightly as true
faith takes its beliefs and true hope its hopes. After
all, what difference should likes and dislikes make
when "all that matters is to be at one with the living
God"? Those we like and those we dislike are equally "at home in the house of the living." We all
belong together. We can all live together in peace,
as soon as we follow our deepest longing and come
home to our heart.

Here, once more, we touch upon the mystery of

the heart. The heart is home. "It all depends on what you mean by home." And one of the characters in Robert Frost's "Death of a Hired Man" answers:

> Home is the place where, when you have to go
>   there,
> They have to take you in.

The other one replies:

> I should have called it
> Something you somehow haven't to deserve.

On both counts the heart is home. In both senses, the heart is where we belong. We belong there as to our proper place, no matter how estranged we have become. And when we are there we belong, because what makes home home is that each belongs to all and all to each.

"Home is where one starts from," says T.S. Eliot. And this is one way of saying that love is not only the end, but the beginning of all. What we find, when we find our heart (and remember, gratefulness is the key), is God's own life within us. It has been going on from "before always," as C.S. Lewis likes to put it. Faith, Hope, and Love are ways in which we explore the life of the Triune God. In Faith we live by every word in which the eternal Word is spelled out in nature and history. In Hope, we let ourselves down into the Silence of the Father, from where the Word comes forth and to where it comes home. In Love we begin to understand, in the Spirit of God's self-understanding, that Word and Silence belong together in action. We come to understand that Belonging is a name of the Triune God. Our heart is rooted in that ultimate belonging. We do not have to earn this, nor do we have to deserve it. It is gratis—pure grace, pure gift. We need only enter into this fullness through gratefulness.

But this gratefulness itself is simply one way of experiencing the life of the Triune God within us. This life springs forth from the Father, the fountain and wellspring of divinity, the ultimate Giver. The total self-gift of the Father is the Son. The Son receives everything from the Father and becomes the turning point in this divine tide of giving. For in the Holy Spirit the Son returns the Father's ultimate giving as ultimate thanksgiving. The Triune God is Giver, Gift, and Thanksgiving. This movement from the Father through the Son in the Spirit back to its Source is what St. Gregory of Nyssa called "the Round Dance of the Blessed Trinity." This is how God prays: by dancing. It is one great celebration of belonging by giving and thanksgiving. We can begin to join that dance in our heart right now through gratefulness. What else could be called life in fullness?

Fullness and Emptiness

This book explores ways of coming more fully alive. Self-fulfillment is a value of which we are conscious today. But we sometimes fail to notice that people who live fulfilled lives are surprisingly selfless. At moments when we experience life in fullness, we are, if not selfless, at least self-forgetful. Don't we all know this from experience?

The fullness for which the human heart longs is always available. But we cannot lay hold of it. We cannot grasp it. Fullness flows into us in the measure in which we become empty. T.S. Eliot states:

> In order to possess what you do not possess
> you must go by the way of dispossession.
> In order to arrive at what you are not
> you must go through the way in which you
> are not.

The preceding chapters speak of gratefulness, faithfulness, prayerfulness, and other aspects of life in fullness. But for fullness in all its forms, emptiness is the necessary condition. With this in mind, I have collected in this final chapter some key words and commented on them briefly. The list is designed to aid the memory of those who have read this book. But here and there it may go further and point beyond any fullness words can convey to an emptiness one can only savor in silence.

Alive

The fact that you are not yet dead is not sufficient proof that you are alive. It takes more than that. It takes courage—above all, the courage to face death. Only one who is alive can die. Aliveness is measured by the ability to die. One who is fully alive is fully able to die. In peak moments of aliveness we are reconciled with death. Deep down within us something tells us that we would die the moment our life reached fulfillment. It is fear of death that prevents us from coming fully alive.

Authority

For a long time now, our society seems to have had a blind spot regarding authority. We blindly assume that human beings are by nature resistant against external authority. The opposite is true. The average person is excessively prone to yield to the pressure of external authority, even when it conflicts with the inner authority of one's conscience. Examples are the atrocities committed by ordinary citizens in Nazi Germany and other dictatorships, or the widespread submission to peer pressure in every society. Given this human weakness, the task of external authority is not to entrench and enforce itself, but rather to build up the inner authority responsibly by constantly encouraging those subject to it to stand on their own two feet. Putting words in print gives them an appearance of authority. This book appeals to one authority only: the reader's own experience. And since it deals with experiences of the heart, it appeals to the authority of the heart. This appeal is a twofold one. It is a question and a challenge. The question is: Does this ring true to your heart's experience? The challenge is: wake up and allow your heart to experience the full range of reality.

Becoming

All we know of being is becoming. Being alive, being grateful, means becoming alive, becoming grateful. Being human means becoming what we are. If you stopped becoming, you would cease to be. Yet, in the process of becoming you cease to be what you were. T.S. Eliot says:

> In order to arrive at what you are not
> You must go through the way in which you are
> not.

The movement of life is the process of becoming. Yet, in this process being and non-being, fullness and emptiness are inextricably one. Remembering this may save us from speaking too glibly about fullness of life.

Belonging

That we belong is a given fact. This means that it is both fact and gift. Belonging is *the* basic fact. All other facts rest on belonging. And it is *the* basic gift. Every other gift celebrates, in its own way, belonging. Belonging is mutual and all-inclusive. Whatever there is belongs to whatever else there is. Every longing somehow longs to realize belonging more fully and thus more fully to be. Because belonging is a fact, we are at home in the world, wherever we may find ourselves. And because belonging is a gift, gratefulness is the right response to life, whatever happens.

Catholic

The literal meaning of "catholic" is "all-embracing." I write as a Catholic Christian because I fail to comprehend how the good news could remain good without being all-embracing. Obviously, this must be taken in the sense of broadness. Jesus excluded no one: "Going into all the world, proclaim the good news to every creature" (Mk 16:15)—not only to all humans! But catholicity must also be taken in the sense of depth. This may be less obvious. Yet the good news is meant to penetrate every layer of reality. Nothing is excluded as being base, unworthy, or profane. Everything within us and around us is to be embraced and transformed. The opposite of catholic is provincial, not Protestant. There are provincial Catholics and catholic Protestants. A person's provincial taste can become catholic through broader exposure to experience. If Catholic with "C" means anything, it means a challenge to Catholics to become truly catholic with "c."

Communication

Although communication is basic to our world, most people have a crippled notion of how it works. They realize that communication aims at communion (mutual understanding, a sense of community, common action). But they fail to see that communion is not only the fruit, but the root of communication. Unless we have already something in common before we start to communicate, communication is impossible. Of course, our common ground expands as we build on it and is enriched in the process. We know that communication broadens and deepens communion. What we tend to forget is that communication also presupposes communion. We need at least the basics of a common language before we can begin to communicate. There could be no communication across the gap of an absolute vacuum. Fortunately, there is no such gap anywhere. At heart, everything hangs together with everything. All communication is rooted in this most basic communion. This insight becomes relevant when we conceive of prayer as communication with God. If there is a gap, God is on our side before we ever start to bridge it. Or, as Thomas Merton put it, prayer does not consist in an effort to get across to God, but in opening our eyes to see that we are already there.

Contemplation

The root meaning of TEMP is measure or measuring. The ending of the word conTEMPlation indicates an ongoing process. And the prefix (*con=cum*=with) tells us that this is a process of measuring two things against each other, pairing them up, putting them together. Thus, contemplation, rightly understood, puts together above and below, seeing and doing. Contemplation translates vision into action, *on earth as it is in heaven*. Action without vision would be confused action. Vision without action would be barren vision. Contemplative vision takes its measure from above. Contemplative action puts order into the chaos below. If we don't want to lose our way, we must keep our eyes on the stars and our feet on the ground. That means we must all be contemplatives.

Death

In death, two events happen at once: being killed and dying. Nothing is more passive than being killed, even if it's merely old age that kills one. But nothing is more active than dying. The verb "dying" does not even have a passive voice. I can say "I'm being killed," but I can't say "I'm being died." Being dyed would make me colorful, not dead. Dying is something I must do. It can't happen unless I give myself willingly to change. I die to what I was and come alive to what I will be. Every moment is, in this sense, a dying into life. Being afraid of death would mean being afraid of life. Learning to die means learning to live.

Divine Life

To speak of divine life as something we know from experience may seem presumptuous. But it would be even more presumptuous to speak about it without knowing it. We either know something by experience, or we do not really know it. There are moments when, altogether gratuitously, we get an inkling of the ground of our being. We realize that we are both at home there and on the way there. Some are bold enough to call this starting point and goal of our heart's journey "God." Nothing else deserves this name. We can call the two poles of this experience God's immanence (closer to me than I am to myself) and God's transcendence (beyond the beyond). If God were merely transcendent, it would indeed be presumptuous to claim any knowledge of God. But a transcendence worthy of God must be so transcendent that it transcends our logical limits of transcendence and is, therefore, perfectly compatible with God's immanence. Would it not be presumptuous to deny this? The fact that I am not simply God needs little proof. And yet, according to Piet Hein,

> Who am I
> To deny
> That, maybe,
> God is me?

Emotions

A good many people are afraid of their emotions, especially in their life of prayer. Emotionalism is indeed a danger, but hardly ever for those who recognize it as a danger. If you are one of those, you may, in fact, need encouragement to give free rein to your feelings. Most of us are apt to repress our emotions. Our upbringing, our social customs, even our teachings on prayer lead us to distrust our emotions, or at least to hide them. That is why people whose emotions flow freely strike us as over-emotional. To dwarfs a normal size person must look like a giant. Emotionalism in prayer is an imbalance that results not from too much feeling, but from too little else. The balance is not redressed by curtailing the emotions, but rather by adding to them our intellectual and moral energy. All we have must go into our prayer. (Note that this includes tact and good taste, two ingredients that will go a long way in keeping the expression of our emotions from disturbing others.)

Faith

To have faith does not primarily mean believing something, but rather believing *in* someone. Faith is trust. It takes courage to trust. The opposite of faith is not disbelief, but distrust, fear. Fear makes us cling to anything within reach. Fear clings even to beliefs. Thus, beliefs can even get in the way of faith. In genuine faith we hold our beliefs firmly, but lightly. We trust in God, not in our particular understanding of God. That is why people of deep faith are one at heart, even though their beliefs may differ widely. When beliefs become more important than faith, even small differences create insurmountable barriers. When we grow in gratefulness, we grow in faith. Gratefulness implies trust in the giver. A grateful person says "Thank you!" and only afterward checks what's inside the gift-wrapping. Faith is the courage to respond gratefully to every given situation, out of trust in the Giver.

Fear

Whenever things go wrong in society, in a person's psyche, or in one's spiritual life, we may be sure that fear in one form or another lies at the root of the trouble. Most of us are fear-ridden people. All of us live in a fear-ridden society. But nothing is gained by this discovery if in addition to all our other fears we now begin to fear fear. Why not rather look at fear as the necessary condition for courage? Piet Hein says:

> To be brave is to behave
> Bravely when your heart is faint.
> So you can be really brave
> Only when you really ain't.

Give-and-Take

"And" is the decisive word in give-and-take. Mere giving is as lifeless as mere taking. If you merely take a breath and stop there, you are dead. And when you merely breathe out and stop there, you are also dead. Life is not giving *or* taking, but give-*and*-take. Breathing is an obvious example, but the same give-and-take can be found wherever there is life. It is the dynamic expression of universal belonging.

Given Reality

We speak of a *given* moment, of *given* facts, of all reality as *given.* The appropriate response to a *given* world is thanksgiving. This has weighty implications. To understand it and to draw the consequences leads to grateful living. And this, in turn, is the key to finding joy.

Giving

The Ibo in Nigeria have a proverb that says, "It is the heart that gives; the fingers just let go." Giving is something only the heart can do. And this is true not only of gift-giving, but of all forms of giving. There are three preeminent forms: giving up, thanksgiving, and forgiving. The heart knows that all belongs to all. And so, when we live from the heart, we are free to give up without fearful clinging. The heart is at home in belonging. And so, when we live from the heart, we celebrate the bond of mutual give-and-take through thanksgiving all we do. The heart fully affirms that all belong to all. And so, when we live from the heart, we forgive from the heart, from that center where offender and offended are one, where healing has its roots. Forgiving is the perfection of giving.

God

Since this book is based on experience and appeals to experience, God comes in as basic to everyone's experience, and only under this aspect. "Restless is our heart." This is a basic fact of human experience. St. Augustine continues the sentence: "Restless is our heart until it rests in God." But this does not mean that we first know God, so that our thirst for God is one among various things worth mentioning. Rather, all we know at first is the restlessness of our heart. And to the direction of our restless yearning, we give the name God. By pooling insights gained by the heart, we can come to know a little bit about God, especially when we listen to great explorers into God. Yet, what matters is never knowledge *about* God, but knowledge of God—as the magnetic North of the human heart.

Gratuitous

> The universe may
> Be as great as they say.
> But it wouldn't be missed
> If it didn't exist.

With a disarming smile, this little jingle by Piet Hein lays bare the gratuitousness of absolutely everything. The universe is gratis. It cannot be earned, nor need it be earned. From this simple fact of experience springs grateful living, grace-filled living. Gratefulness is the heart's full response to the gratuitousness of all that exists. And gratefulness makes us graceful in a double sense. In gratefulness we open ourselves to this gratuitous universe and so we become fully graced with it. And in doing so we learn to move gracefully with its flow, as in a universal dance.

Heart

Whenever we speak of the heart, we mean the whole person. Only at heart are we whole. The heart stands for that center of our being where we are one with ourselves, one with all others, one with God. The heart is ever restless in its quest for God, and yet, deep down, it is ever at home in God. To live from the heart means to live out of the fullness of this longing and belonging. And that means to live fully.

Hope

There is a close connection between hope and hopes, but we must not confuse the two. We set our hopes on something we can imagine. But hope is open for the unimaginable. The opposite of hopes is hopelessness. The opposite of hope is despair. One can cling desperately to one's hopes. But even in a hopeless situation hope remains open for surprise. It is surprise that links hope with gratefulness. To the grateful heart every gift is surprising. Hope is openness for surprise.

Humility

Today, humility is not a popular virtue; but only because it is misunderstood. Many think that humility is a pious lie committed by people who claim to be worse than they know themselves to be, so that they can secretly pride themselves in being so humble. In truth, however, to be humble means simply to be earthy. The word "humble" is related to "humus," the vegetable mold of top soil. It is also related to human and humor. If we accept and embrace the earthiness of our human condition (and a bit of humor helps) we shall find ourselves doing so with humble pride. In our best moments humility is simply pride that is too grateful to look down on anyone.

I

It is no mere coincidence that the personal pronoun "I" in the English language cannot be distinguished by its sound from the word "eye" for the organ of sight. This adds an additional layer of meaning to the English version of Meister Eckhardt's famous saying, "The eye by which I see God is the very eye by which God sees me." When we understand our I in this sense, we give it its deepest meaning and escape from the prison of the individualistic little self.

Individual

It is necessary to distinguish clearly between individual and person. We are individuals by being separate and distinct from others. We become persons by relating to others. Born as so many human individuals, we grow up to become human persons. In order to accomplish this, we need others. Individuals differ in the degree to which they have become persons because their relationships to others differ in complexity and intensity. As our relationships to others unfold and change, they influence our relationship to God and self. Overemphasis on individuality leads to alienation by denying our deep mutual interdependence. As one becomes a person, individuality is at one and the same time enhanced and transcended.

Joy

Ordinary happiness depends on happenstance. Joy is that extraordinary happiness that is independent of what happens to us. Good luck can make us happy, but it cannot give us lasting joy. The root of joy is gratefulness. We tend to misunderstand the link between joy and gratefulness. We notice that joyful people are grateful and suppose that they are grateful for their joy. But the reverse is true: their joy springs from gratefulness. If one has all the good luck in the world, but takes it for granted, it will not give one joy. Yet even bad luck will give joy to those who manage to be grateful for it. We hold the key to lasting happiness in our own hands. For it is not joy that makes us grateful; it is gratitude that makes us joyful.

Jesus Christ

In speaking not merely of Jesus, or merely of Christ, but of Jesus Christ, we stress the tension between two points of reference. One is in time: the historic Jesus. The other is timeless: the Christ-reality in Him and in all of us. We must maintain the creative tension between these two aspects, for if we allow it to snap, our relationship to Jesus Christ will be polarized. We will either be unable to look beyond the historic frame of reference, or else run the risk of losing our historic anchorage altogether. The historic Jesus provides an objective standard for the life of Christians. This prevents their awareness of the Christ within them from drifting off into mere subjectivity. Yet the historic Jesus is merely one point of reference in genuine encounter with Jesus Christ. The other is expressed in the words, "Christ lives in me" (Gal 2:20).

Knowing

"Knowledge is power," we say. And we think of it as power we can wield to achieve our purpose. Wisdom, in contrast, ripens only when we are gradually overpowered by meaning. In the biblical notion of "knowing" these two are reconciled. In the give-and-take of sexual knowledge, which provides the biblical model for knowing, we are both empowered and overpowered; we come to know by being known. This give-and-take can be understood as a giving and receiving of thanks. The bond that unites giver and thanksgiver is one of deep mutual recognition.

Leisure

We tend to think of leisure as the privilege of those who can afford to take time off. But leisure is a virtue, not a luxury. Leisure is the virtue of those who take their time in order to give to each task as much time as it deserves to take. Giving and taking, play and work, meaning and purpose are perfectly balanced in leisure. We learn to live fully in the measure in which we learn to live leisurely.

Love

We allow the experience of falling in love to shape our concept of love in general. This puts us on the wrong track. Passionate attraction is indeed an important instance of love. But it is far too specific a type of loving to serve as model for love in general. When we ask for characteristics of love applicable to each and all of its forms, we find at least two: a sense of belonging and wholehearted acceptance of that belonging with all its implications. These two characteristics are typical for every kind of love, from love of one's country to love of one's pets, while passionate attraction is typical only of falling in love. Love is a wholehearted "yes" to belonging. When we fall in love, our sense of belonging is overpowering, our "yes" is spontaneous and blissful. Falling in love challenges us to rise in love. We can broaden the scope of our "yes," say it under less favorable conditions, and draw out its consequences all the way to love our enemies. Since August 6, 1945, no one can deny that all of us belong together in this spaceship Earth. "When you are in the same boat with your worst enemy, will you drill a hole into his side of the boat?" asks Elissa Melamed.

Meaning

We humans cannot find peace of heart unless we find meaning in life. Meaning is that in which our hearts find rest. We never achieve meaning as one achieves a purpose by hard work. It is always received as pure gift. And yet we must *give* meaning to our lives. How can we do this? Through gratefulness. Gratefulness is the inner gesture of *giving* meaning to our life by *receiving* life as gift. The deepest meaning of any given moment lies in the fact that it is given. Gratefulness recognizes, acknowledges, and celebrates this meaning.

Mystic Experience

If we think of it as an experience of communion with Ultimate Reality, we have a fair working definition of mystic experience. We will do well not to introduce the term "God" into our definition. Not all people feel comfortable calling Ultimate Reality "God." But all of us, regardless of terminology, can experience moments of overwhelming, limitless belonging, moments of universal communion. Those are our own mystic moments. The men and women we call mystics differ from the rest of us merely by giving these experiences the place they deserve in everyone's life. What counts is not the frequency or intensity of mystic experiences, but the influence we allow them to have on our life. By accepting our mystic moments with all they offer and demand, we become the mystics we are meant to be. After all, a mystic is not a special kind of human being, but every human being is a special kind of mystic.

Nature/Supernature

The distinction between natural and supernatural is valid. Yet no one can separate the two; no one can draw a line between them. Nature and supernature are not two different realms of reality, two different layers of the universe. One and the same reality will be natural or supernatural, depending on how we approach it. What we take hold of, physically or intellectually, will always be the natural. By taking hold of it, we limit it. The supernatural is limitless. We must let it take hold of us. A bucket full of water from the river is not a bucket full of river, no matter how much water it may hold. But by diving off the bank into the water, we dive into the river, no matter how far that spot may be from the source. No matter where we immerse ourselves in the stream of reality, we will be in touch with the supernatural source of all that is natural.

Nothing

Whatever we encounter is either thing or nothing. In his poem "The Snow Man," Wallace Stevens distinguishes between "the nothing that isn't there and the nothing that is." Meaning is "the nothing that is." Meaning is no thing. And yet the nothing that is meaning is far more important to us humans than all things taken together.

Openness

Observing the way an anemone opens to the morning light, Rilke asks: And we, when are *we* ever fully open to receive? Openness in this sense stands for a basic attitude toward life, for a readiness to receive life in fullness. But is openness in itself fullness or emptiness? Think, for example, of hope's openness for surprise. Hope is fully open only when it is drained empty of all hopes. Even the shape of the letter O, the initial of openness, is ambiguous: the *empty* circle is the symbol of *fullness*. The interplay between fullness and emptiness pivots on openness.

Opportunity

Until we recognize the pre-eminent role that opportunity plays in the scheme of things, our notion of gratefulness must remain deficient. Whatever exists within this given word is gift. But the gift within every gift is opportunity.

Most of the time, this means opportunity to enjoy. Sometimes it means opportunity to labor, to suffer, even to die. Unless we wake up to the countless opportunities to enjoy life, how can we expect to be awake when the opportunity comes to serve life? Those who realize that the gift within every gift is opportunity will not think of gratitude as passive. Gratefulness is the gallantry of a heart ready to rise to the opportunity a given moment offers.

Paradox

Nicholas of Cusa expressed what the human heart had always surmised: all opposites coincide in God. This insight has weighty implications for any attempt to speak about divine realities. The closer we come to saying something worthwhile, the more likely that paradox will be the only way to express it. "When I am weak, then I am strong" (2 Cor 12:10). "In losing one's life one will find it" (Mt 10:39). "In spite of that, we call this Friday good" (T.S. Eliot, *Four Quartets*).

Peak Experience

Abraham Maslow, who put the Peak Experience on the map of psychology, insisted that it could in no way be distinguished from mystic experience as described by the mystics. And yet, most (if not all) of us have Peak Experiences, moments in which we are overwhelmed by a sense of belonging, of universal wholeness and holiness, moments in which everything makes sense. Acceptance is a word often used in describing Peak Experiences. For a moment that seems outside time, we feel fully accepted and can fully accept all that is. Gratefulness pervades every aspect of these peaks. The religiousness at the core of a person's religion is fueled by those moments of overwhelming gratefulness. One's religion is seen as valid in the light of those experiences of heightened awareness. It is measured by standards glimpsed from those peaks of grateful acceptance. That is why we can call gratefulness the root of religion.

Prayer

We must distinguish prayer from prayers. Saying prayers is one activity among others. But prayer is an attitude of the heart that can transform every activity. We cannot say prayers at all times, but we ought to "pray without ceasing" (1 Thess 5:17). That means we ought to keep our heart open for the meaning of life. Gratefulness does this, moment by moment. Gratefulness is, therefore, prayerfulness. Moments in which we drink deeply from the source of meaning are moments of prayer, whether we call them so or not. There is no human heart that does not pray, at least in deep dreams that nourish life with meaning. What matters is prayer, not prayers. But prayers are the poetry of prayerful living. Just as poetry gives expression to one's aliveness and makes one more alive, so prayers give expression to one's prayerfulness and make one more prayerful.

Questions

To prevent questions from weighing us down, we must raise them. The longer we wait, the heavier they get, like a thatched roof in the rain. People who are afraid of raising questions run the risk of getting crushed under them. When we raise a question all the way, we find that the answer to every "Why?" is "Yes!" This sets us free. But even the raising of questions to lesser degrees is freeing. Questions can free us, e.g., from misconceptions, above all from the misconception that we can know anything unquestioningly. For this reason, we have made an effort in these pages to question basic terms for what they really mean—terms like communication, belonging, or meaning. Basic terms are the foundation on which logical reasoning rests. When the foundations are slightly off, the superstructure may suddenly topple over. Keen questioning is no luxury.

Religion

The various religions are so many ways of being religious. It is this underlying religiousness we have in mind when we speak of religion as distinct from the religions. We would need an action word, a verb, to express what religion is all about. But, while we have "religion, religious, and religiously," we cannot say that someone is "religioning." Praying is the verb that goes with religion. Praying (in the widest sense) is what keeps religious experience from drying up into nothing but religious structures. Experience is the starting point of religion. Inevitably, intellect, will, and emotions grapple, each in its own way, with the experience of ultimate belonging. The intellect interprets the experience, and so we get religious doctrine. The will acknowledges the implications, and that accounts for the ethical side of religion. The emotions celebrate the experience by means of ritual. But a religion is not automatically religious. Those three main areas of every religion are always prone to shrivel up into dogmatism, legalism, and ritualism unless they are continually rerooted in live experience. This process is prayer. Prayer puts religion into the religions.

Silence

There is a negative meaning to silence and a positive one. Negatively, silence means the absence of sound or word. In these pages we focus on its positive meaning. Silence is the matrix from which word is born, the home to which word returns through understanding. Word (in contrast to chatter) does not break the silence. In a genuine word, silence comes to word. In genuine understanding, word comes home into silence. For those who know only the world of words, silence is mere emptiness. But our silent heart knows the paradox: the emptiness of silence is inexhaustibly rich; all the words in the world are merely a trickle of its fullness.

Sin

In our day and age, the word "sin" is so prone to be misunderstood that it has become quite useless. The reality once called sin is still with us, however, and so our time had to find its own term for it. What other ages called sin, we call alienation. Living language hit upon an apt word here. Alienation suggests an uprootedness from one's true self, from others, from God (or whatever else ultimately matters), and all this with one word. The word "sin," too, suggests uprooting and separation. It is related to the word "asunder." Sin tears asunder the wholeness in which all belongs together. Sin alienates. An action is sinful to the degree to which it causes alienation. Without alienation there is no sin. Drawing the consequences could prove liberating for many, indicting for others. It could mean a significant shift of emphasis in ethics from a pre-occupation with private perfection to social responsibility. It could help us see that in our time "working out our salvation" means overcoming alienation in all its forms. The contemporary term for salvation is belonging. The path from alienation to belonging is the path fron sin to salvation.

Surprise

For Plato, philosophy was a loving dedication to wisdom. Hence, surprise and the ability to be surprised were for him the beginning of philosophy. It is through the capacity for surprise that wisdom surpasses mere cleverness. Cleverness is prepared and will not be surprised by the unexpected. But wisdom, as Piet Hein sees it, is prepared to be surprised even by the expected.

> Half a truth is often aired
> And often proved correct:
> It's sensible to be prepared
> For what you don't expect.
>
> The other half is minimized
> Or totally neglected:
> It's wiser still to be surprised
> By what you most expected.

To recognize that everything is surprising is the first step toward recognizing that everything is gift. The wisdom that begins with surprise is the wisdom of a grateful heart.

Thanksgiving

On a superficial level, the giving of thanks is merely a social convention. Its forms vary greatly. In some societies the absence of all verbal expressions of thanks indicates not a lack of gratitude, but rather a deeper awareness of mutual belonging than our society has. To the people in question, an expression like "thank you" would seem as inappropriate as tipping family members would seem to us. The more we lose the sense of all belonging to one big family, the more we must explicitly express that belonging when it is actualized in some give-and-take. To give thanks means to give expression to mutual belonging. Genuine thanksgiving comes from the heart where we are rooted in universal belonging.

Wholehearted thanksgiving engages the whole person. The intellect recognizes the gift as gift. Thanksgiving presupposes thinking. The will, in its turn, acknowledges the interdependence of the giver and thanksgiver. And the emotions celebrate the joy of that mutual belonging. Only when intellect, will and emotions join together does thanksgiving become genuine, i.e., wholehearted.

Truth

What our heart longs for is truth, but what we can express are merely truths. Truth is one. But its countless aspects can be expressed in conflicting truths. Their limitations bring them into conflict. All we can grasp of the truth are limited truths. But grasping is not the only attitude we can adopt toward truth. Instead of grasping for truths, we can allow the truth to grasp us. It is one thing to take a bucket full of water out of the ocean. To swim in the ocean is quite a different thing. The truths we can grasp are necessarily limited as our grasp is limited. But the truth to which we give ourselves is limitless and one. The truths tend to divide us, but the truth that upholds us unites.

Understanding

It is through understanding that we find meaning. In every meaningful situation there must be something that *has* meaning. Word is the broadest sense. There must also be Silence, the horizon of Word, the mysterious matrix from which Word emerges. And there must be Understanding or else the meaning never arrives. Word, Silence, and Understanding are the three dimensions of meaning as it were. But what happens when we understand? We give ourselves to the Word so wholeheartedly that it can take hold of us. When the Word takes us home into the Silence from where it has come, we understand. But going along with the Word is something that requires effort. It means doing what the Word sends us to do. When we listen so deeply that we hear where the Word sends us and fulfill that mission, we understand. It is in doing that we understand. Anything else is not *under*standing, but at best an attempt to *over*stand. It is not possible to understand swimming unless we get wet. If we want to understand life, we must live.

Usefulness

Quite unawares, one can get trapped in a world in which only the useful counts. The life expectancy of people who make usefulness their highest value drops abruptly after retirement. Common sense tells us that aliveness is not measured in degrees of usefulness but of enjoyment. Yet public opinion tries to persuade us that we do not need what is of no use. The contrary is true. What we need most urgently is not what we can use, but what we can enjoy. This distinction is crucial. Our deepest need is not use but enjoyment. The most enjoyable things in life are superfluous—music, for instance, or mountain climbing, or a kiss. "Superfluity," as the word suggests, is an abounding overflow after the vessel of mere utility has been filled to the brim (like the stone vessels at the wedding feast in Cana of Galilee—Jn 2:8). In the word "affluence" the same idea of flowing is present, but only influx is what counts. In a utilitarian society there is only usefulness and more usefulness without the sparkling overflow that keeps it

from getting stagnant. Enjoyment is not measured by what flows in, but by what flows over.
The smaller we make the vessel of our need for
use, the sooner we get the overflow we need for
delight. This was well understood by the beggar
who said, "Two coppers I had; for one I bought
me a bun, for one daffodils."

Vacation

If it were not for vacations, our schools would
hardly deserve to be called schools. Traced back
to its Greek origin, the term "school" means a
place of leisure. Nowadays, this sounds like a
joke. But the joke is on us. Originally, schools
were conceived as places where people had
leisure enough to find themselves. In our time,
many young people need to take a year off from
the rat-race of school in order to find themselves. Schools are now geared toward purpose
rather than meaning, toward know-how rather
than wisdom. What enriched your own life
more, the useful things you did at school or the
enjoyable things you did on vacation? For most
of us, vacation means fullness of life. Yet the
word is relegated to vacuum and vacancy.
Here, too, fullness and emptiness are closely
related. "Be still and see that I am God!" (Ps
46:10). In the emptiness of silence you will find
My fullness. Instead of "Be still," St. Jerome
translates, "Make a vacation!"

Way

In the earliest days, men and women who believed in Jesus Christ were simply known as followers of the Way (Acts 9:2). Only later were they labeled Christians (Acts 11:26). To escape being paralyzed by labels, one must continually trust the dynamic experience of being on the way. When Jesus says, "I am the Way" (Jn 14:6), we would limit his claim pitifully by thinking of one way among a thousand others. This cannot be the meaning of his word. Rather, whosoever is "on the way" to God is on the way of Jesus whose name means "God saves." And whoever follows the deepest longing of the human heart is "on the way." It matters little what label we give to that way. Holding on to the sign post does not mean "being on the way," even if that street sign bears the right label. What matters is walking. All those who move forward are on the way. But this means finding one's way by leaving the way behind with every step forward.

Work/Play

Human activity is of two kinds: work and play. We work in order to achieve some useful purpose. But we play for mere enjoyment. Play is meaningful in itself. We can become so purpose-ridden in our work that even after work we can no longer play; we can at best give ourselves another work-out. Usefulness is crowding out enjoyment. What a waste of time!

But we can rescue work from becoming mere drudgery. We can learn to work playfully. That means doing our work not only for its useful results, but also for the enjoyment we can find in it all along when we do it mindfully, gratefully. Grateful work is playful work, leisurely work. Only leisurely work is, in the long run, efficient. Only when we work playfully are we fully alive.

Wonderment

G.K. Chesterton reminds us in one of his puns that wonders will never be lacking in this world of ours; what is lacking is wonderment. We need not look beyond natural laws for wonders. Natural laws themselves are wonderful enough and worth wondering. Piet Hein reminds us:

> We glibly talk of nature's laws
> But do things have a natural cause?
> Blackearth becoming yellow crocus
> Is undiluted hocus-pocus.

If you can't wonder at what is natural, what would it take to make you wonder? As long as you are full of yourself, you are incapable of wonderment, and life seems empty. But in wonderment you lose yourself. "Lost, all lost in wonder," you are emptied of your little self, and suddenly you realize how wonderful everything is, how full of wonder, how full.

Word

When we find something meaningful, we say it "speaks" to us, it has a message. In this sense, any thing, person, or situation can be understood as word. Karl Rahner, who has taught me by his writings, thinks of word as a sign that embodies its meaning. Raimundo Panikkar, who has taught me not only by his writings but by his friendship, explores in his own way how word, silence, and understanding are related. What most determines my use of "word" in this book is the basic biblical truth that "God speaks." If God speaks, the whole universe and everything in it is word. This is the biblical way of saying that everything makes sense the moment we listen with the heart. We will find this to be true if we have courage to listen. That courage is called faith. The listening is called obedience. That term comes from the Latin *ob-audiens* and means thoroughly listening. Its opposite is *ab-surdus*, which means thoroughly deaf. We can escape from absurdity by learning to listen to the word in everything we encounter.

X

Is it merely by chance that X has two contradictory functions? X marks the spot, and X crosses out whatever is found on that spot. With two strokes, X expresses the paradox contained in the word NOWHERE. By simply making a little space inside of nowhere, we can transform it into NOW HERE. X marks the spot where we find ourselves here and now in the midst of nowhere. This puts us on the spot. Or shall we say it puts us on the crossroads? X is a cross in disguise, a cross that stands on two legs, instead of one. When we allow ourselves to be put on the spot, we stand at "the point of intersection of the timeless with time," "at the still point of the turning world" (T.S. Eliot, *Four Quartets*) now here and nowhere. This book is about life in fullness. X marks the spot where fullness and emptiness are one.

Yes

How often we say "Yes!" And yet most of the time we say a conditional "yes"—"yes, if . . ." or "yes, but . . ." Most of the time there are strings attached to our "yes." But now and then we get carried away like kites in a great wind and say an unconditional "yes." At that moment we realize that "yes" is the answer to every "why?" and suddenly everything makes sense. When e.e. cummings thanks God "for everything which is natural which is infinite which is yes," he has this limitless affirmation in mind. So does St. Paul, when he calls Jesus Christ the great Yes (2 Cor 1:20). The "yes" of the human heart is our full response to the "faithfulness at the heart of all things." In saying this "yes," we become what we are. Our true Self is "Yes."

You

The relationship between I and Thou has been brilliantly explored by Ferdinand Ebner and Martin Buber. But it took them volumes to say what e.e. cummings sings in a single line of a love poem: "I am through You so I." (Not only am I through you so happy, so alive, but "so I.") In moments in which I can sing this line with conviction, I know that fulfillment is found when I am completely empty.

Zero

The very shape of zero, written as 0, expresses emptiness. But the full circle also signifies fullness. Zero stands for nothing, but by adding zero to a number we can multiply it tenfold, a hundredfold, a thousandfold. Gratefulness gives fullness to life by adding nothing. Understanding 0 by becoming 0—that's what gratefulness is all about. Anyone who understands the preceding sentence no longer knows how to read it aloud. That's one good reason for *writing* this book.